D1759730

Quantitative Applications in the Social Sciences

A SAGE PUBLICATIONS SERIES

Quantitative Applications in the Social Sciences

A SAGE PUBLICATIONS SERIES

BRIEF CONTENTS

DETAILED CONTENTS

ABOUT THE AUTHORS

Lingxin Hao is Professor of Sociology at the Johns Hopkins University. She was a 2002–2003 Visiting Scholar at the Russell Sage Foundation and a 2007 Resident Fellow at the Spencer Foundation. Her areas of specialization include the family and public policy, social inequality, immigration, quantitative methods, and advanced statistics. The focus of her research is on social inequality, emphasizing the effects of structural, institutional, and contextual forces in addition to individual and family factors. Her research tests hypotheses derived from sociological and economic theories using advanced statistical methods and large national survey datasets. Her articles have appeared in various journals, including *Sociological Methodology*, *Sociological Methods and Research*, *Quality and Quantity*, *American Journal of Sociology*, *Social Forces*, *Sociology of Education*, *Social Science Research*, and *International Migration Review*. She received her PhD in sociology in 1990 from the University of Chicago.

Daniel Q. Naiman is Professor and Chair of the Department of Applied Mathematics and Statistics at the Johns Hopkins University. He was elected as a Fellow of the Institute of Mathematical Statistics in 1997 and was an Erskine Fellow at the University of Canterbury in 2005. Much of his mathematical research has been focused on geometric and computational methods for multiple testing. He has collaborated on papers applying statistics in a variety of areas: bioinformatics, econometrics, environmental health, genetics, hydrology, and microbiology. His articles have appeared in various journals, including *Annals of Statistics, Bioinformatics, Biometrika, Human Heredity, Journal of Multivariate Analysis, Journal of the American Statistical Association,* and *Science*. He received his PhD in mathematics in 1982 from the University of Illinois at Urbana–Champaign.

SERIES EDITOR'S INTRODUCTION

Social inequality has been addressed by classical and modern social theorists in qualitative research and in quantitative social research: Inequality is perhaps the central topic in social science.

The quantitative assessment of social inequality is the subject of Lingxin Hao and Daniel Naiman's wide-ranging monograph, complementing their previous QASS monograph on quantile regression. The authors are concerned particularly with comparisons of inequality—for example, of income or wealth—across societies, among social groups within a society, and over time. The topic is developed from first principles, presupposing only a modest background in mathematics and statistics.

Hao and Naiman describe the relatively well-known and widely used Lorenz curve and Gini index of inequality and systematically develop the rationale of and criteria for summary measures of inequality more generally, but they emphasize methods that compare entire distributions. Moving beyond a focus on averages, for example, the authors link the study of inequality to quantile regression, a method that traces how the conditional distribution of a response variable such as income, not just its center, changes with explanatory variables such as gender, race, or education.

Quantitative research on social inequality is often based on complex social surveys in which sampling errors are nonnegligible, and for which simple textbook methods of inference based on independent random sampling are inappropriate. Hao and Naiman consequently describe methods of statistical inference for measures of inequality suitable for such data, linking their discussion to available software. Their treatment includes both standard asymptotic methods and an approach based on the bootstrap.

I expect that Hao and Naiman's wide-ranging, accessible, and thorough treatment of methods for assessing social inequality will be of great value to researchers working in this centrally important area of social science.

Editor's note: This monograph was begun under the direction of the previous series editor, Tim Futing Liao.

—*John Fox*
Series Editor

ACKNOWLEDGMENTS

The authors and Sage gratefully acknowledge the contributions of the following reviewers:

Glenn Firebaugh, *Pennsylvania State University*

Stephen Jenkins, *University of Essex*

CHAPTER 1. INTRODUCTION

This is the second volume of a two-book series on inequality studies. The first, *Quantile Regression* (Hao & Naiman, 2007), establishes the link between quantile regression models and inequality studies. This book has two goals. First, it reviews a set of widely used summary inequality measures, and the less-known relative distribution method, provides the basic rationale behind each, and discusses their interconnections. Second, the book introduces a technique to perform model-based decomposition of inequality over time using quantile regression. This model-based approach enables us to estimate two different contributors to changes in inequality between two time points. One contributor is the compositional change of the covariates, and the other is the change in the conditional distribution of the response given the covariates.

Social inequality is at the core of the social science discipline. Sociologists, for example, have long been interested in both individual and group inequalities in resources and opportunities shaped by social structure (Blau, 1977) and have addressed both theoretical and methodological implications of summary measures of inequality (Allison, 1978). Numerous empirical studies have been conducted on patterns, trends, causes, and consequences of inequality in resources and in well-being. There is an extensive literature on how to measure inequality. Researchers have created a large number of summary inequality measures and have applied them to empirical research: the Gini coefficient, the coefficient of variation, the logarithm of variance, the Theil inequality index, the Atkinson index, and the generalized entropy, to name a few. Introductions to these measures, however, are not always connected to notions that social scientists are familiar with. In addition, the relationships among the measures are not explicitly stated. For example, we may want to know why the Gini coefficient emphasizes the middle portion of the distribution, how we should compare the Gini coefficient with the generalized entropy, or how to reconcile the use of multiple inequality measures. Moreover, in trend studies, both the population composition and the distribution of an attribute often change simultaneously. It is therefore necessary to separate compositional change from change in the conditional distribution. This book seeks to address these issues.

We define inequality in terms of equality—the absence of inequality. Equality means even distribution of resources, in which everyone in a population gets an equal amount (in absolute terms), or an equal share (in relative terms), of a resource such as income or wealth or a well-being measure such as health. Equality seldom exists in the real world. Existing

1

inequality research seeks to quantify the degree of inequality. Note that equality and equity are distinct concepts. Equity concerns the welfare of the whole society and allows that the allocation of resources need not be equal. If some members of the society are better-off and no one is worse-off, the total welfare of the society is considered greater. In subsequent chapters, we will revisit the distinction between inequality and social welfare.

We conceive of inequality as distributional differences between societies, between social groups, or between time periods. Inequality of a population attribute can be measured in various ways, including summary inequality measures. Using summary inequality measures, such as the Gini coefficient or Theil's index, researchers compare the shapes of two or more distributions. Other inequality measures quantify other differences between two or more distributions, including the central location (the mean or median), the scale (the standard deviation or interquartile range), and the shape (the skewness or peakedness). For instance, in a comparison of the income distribution of today with the one a decade ago, three scenarios can illustrate the shifts in these properties of distribution: First, every household gained a fixed-amount increase, resulting in a pure positive location shift and a decrease in summary measures of inequality (e.g., a lower Gini coefficient). Second, every household received a fixed-percentage increase, resulting in a positive location shift as well as a scale increase, and no change in a particular set of summary inequality measures (e.g., no change in the Gini coefficient). Third, the households at the bottom half experienced a smaller percentage gain than those in the upper half (as has occurred with U.S. income distribution since 1973), resulting in a positive location shift, a scale increase, a greater right skewness, and an increase in summary inequality measures (e.g., a higher Gini coefficient). The interrelationships among different summary inequality measures can be made clearer by relating them with location, scale, and shape shifts.

The primary objective of this book is to provide the most basic foundation for measuring inequality from the perspective of distributional properties. We introduce three subsets of inequality measures: (1) summary measures, (2) quantile-based measures, and (3) relative-distribution-based measures. With the large body of literature of inequality measures, it is a difficult decision which to include and which to omit. The monograph does not include poverty and concentration measures or mobility indexes. We take the point of view that the most important variables to consider are continuous, so we only consider the inequality that is measured based on continuous variables. Given that most social scientists are familiar with and comfortable in talking about distributional properties (e.g., mean/median, variance, skewness, and kurtosis), we build on basic familiarity with these concepts. We present key properties of all the inequality measures that we include and discuss their strengths and weaknesses. At the same time, we avoid making judgments regarding which measures are superior.

Several investigators have introduced methodology for decomposing sources of inequality between time periods. Isolation of the conditional distributional change from the covariate compositional change in trend studies has been achieved using non-model-based decomposition methods (Cowell, 2000). An alternative approach is the regression-model-based decomposition (Oaxaca, 1973) and its modern treatment with residuals (Juhn, Murphy, & Pierce, 1993). This method is limited because it is confined to the conditional mean framework. The pioneering development in density decomposition relates summary inequality measures directly to the density functions they represent (Autor, Katz, & Kearney, 2005; DiNardo, Forth, & Lemieux, 1996). The quantile-regression-based decomposition approach (Machado & Mata, 2005), which builds on quantile regression analysis (Hao & Naiman, 2007; Koenker, 2005), offers a more flexible method for model-based decomposition. Continuing with the earlier QASS *Quantile Regression* (Hao & Naiman, 2007), this book introduces how quantile regression can be used to identify the composition component and the conditional distribution component in trends of inequality measures.

Throughout the book, we discuss issues regarding the measurement and analysis of inequality, through a quantity associated with the distribution of a continuous response variable Y. Chapter 2 introduces location, scale, and shape shifts between distributions and how these shifts manifest themselves in the probability density function (PDF), cumulative distribution function (CDF), and quantile function. The chapter also introduces the standard Lorenz curve and the generalized Lorenz curve and the relationship between the quantile function and the Lorenz curve. Chapter 3 reviews a set of widely used summary inequality measures. Chapter 4 discusses how choices among summary inequality measures can be made based on five principles and how Lorenz dominance can be used to guide the selection of a minimum set of inequality measures for comparing populations. Chapter 5 discusses relative distribution methods as a flexible tool for measuring and analyzing inequality. In Chapter 6, we discuss the conditions under which the asymptotic inference method or the bootstrap inference method should be used and how to obtain the standard errors and confidence intervals for inequality measures based on survey data. Chapter 7 is devoted to non-model-based and quantile-regression-model-based decomposition of inequality trends. The final chapter gives a real-world research example that examines inequality in household income and wealth in 1991 and 2001, employing most of the techniques discussed in the book.

Examples of outcome variables Y for inequality study arise in several areas. One might be interested in economic well-being, which would lead to investigation of income or wealth, academic achievement, which could be measured by standardized test scores, or health, as described by a quantity such as the body mass index. Throughout the book, we use household income as an example for variables with positive values and household wealth as an example for variables with negative, zero, or positive values. While the unit of analysis can be individuals, families, or households, we choose households because these resources are shared among household members, and we are interested in the well-being level of the household as a whole. Household characteristics are measured by the race, education, and age of the household head, household type, and place of residence. Comparisons of income or wealth distributions are made between social groups or the U.S. population between two times. The Survey of Income and Program Participation (SIPP) 1991 and 2001, during the period of rising inequality in the United States, provide the empirical data for illustrations (these data are also used in the first volume of the two-book series). The data, Stata routines, and chapter appendixes for proofs are posted at the authors' Web site for this book (www.ams.jhu.edu/~hao/INEQ_Book).

CHAPTER 2. PDFs, CDFs, QUANTILE FUNCTIONS, AND LORENZ CURVES

The purpose of Chapter 2 is to lay a foundation for the connection between distributional properties (such as the central tendency, dispersion, skewness, and kurtosis) of a population attribute and inequality measures in a broad sense. We use hypothetical data to illustrate how a change in the distribution such as a location shift, a scale shift, or a shape shift is reflected in the changes in mean, variance, skewness, and kurtosis. We then briefly review probability density functions (PDFs) and cumulative distribution functions (CDFs), introduce quantile functions, and then introduce Lorenz curves, basing them on quantile functions. Lorenz curves provide a common basis that can unite many summary inequality measures.

Ranks, PDFs, CDFs, and Moments

Throughout the book, we use income as an example of the attribute of interest. The observed income data for an individual i is denoted by y_i, so that the totality of observed income data (without ordering) will be denoted by $y_1, \ldots, y_n$. The ordered values $y_{(1)}, \ldots, y_{(n)}$ are obtained when individuals' incomes are sorted from the lowest to the highest. An individual's income *rank* refers to the position that the individual's income takes among the ordered values. Ranks are useful for analyzing and studying distributional properties. In his 1973 "Parade of Dwarfs," Pen envisioned incomes as heights and individuals as marching in order from shortest to tallest. The march takes on the appearance of a nondecreasing curve. In the "Parade of Dwarfs," the dwarfs (the very low-income individuals) and the giants (the very high-income individuals) capture one's attention. All the basic tools that we use, including PDFs, CDFs, quantile functions, and Lorenz curves, can be based on ranked data.

The PDF of individual income Y, f_Y, uses the area under the curve to describe the relative frequency of ranges of income values and completely describes the probability distribution of income. The CDF, F_Y, describes cumulative probabilities; that is, $F_Y(y)$ gives the probability that income is less than y, for any given income y. For purely illustrative purposes, we generate a hypothetical income variable $Y^{(0)}$ whose distribution is symmetric (we refer to this as the "original" data), and we present its PDF and CDF in Figure 2.1. The p on the CDF corresponding to a y in Figure 2.1b expresses the area under the PDF up to y in Figure 2.1a. Visually, we can see where the central location lies, how dispersed (scale) the distribution is, and whether the shape of the distribution is symmetric or skewed. For a normal distribution as shown in Figure 2.1, the shape of the PDF is reflection symmetric and the shape of the CDF is rotation symmetric.

To better understand distributional properties, we consider how a location shift, a scale shift, and a shape shift are captured by PDFs and CDFs. First, location shifts result from adding or subtracting a fixed amount of resource to every member of the population. When $Y^{(1)}$ is obtained by adding some constant a to $Y^{(0)}$, so that $Y^{(1)} = a + Y^{(0)}$, we refer to $Y^{(1)}$ as a location shift of $Y^{(0)}$. For example, when each person receives the same additional amount of income, the result is a positive location shift. On the other hand, taxing every person the same amount gives rise to a negative location shift. Second, scale shifts result from increasing or decreasing everyone's resource by a fixed percentage. If $Y^{(2)}$ is obtained by multiplying $Y^{(0)}$ by some positive constant c, so that $Y^{(2)} = cY^{(0)}$, we refer to $Y^{(2)}$ as a scale shift of $Y^{(0)}$. For example, each person may receive a fixed percentage increase in income from his or her employers. Third, shape shifts result from increasing or decreasing the resource of the members of a population by different amounts. Starting with a symmetric distribution, if individuals in the upper half of the distribution receive a greater percentage raise than those in the lower half, the distribution will become right skewed; conversely if individuals with higher pay are subjected to a higher tax rate, the distribution will become left skewed. Thus, multiplication of individuals' incomes by factors depending on individuals' incomes can result in skewness shifts.

Figure 2.2 compares the PDFs and CDFs of the four shifts (location, scale, right-skewed, and left-skewed) with those of the original normal distribution of income. To aid comparisons, we plot these functions using a common x and y range. The five subgraphs in Figure 2.2a show that (1) the positive location shift moves the PDF to the right; (2) the scale shift moves the PDF to the right and widens its spread; (3) the right-skewed shift moves the PDF to the right and widens the spread more in the upper half than in the lower half; and (4) the left-skewed shift moves the PDF to the left and contracts the spread more in the upper half than in the lower half. After the location shift and the scale shift, the PDF remains symmetric, but after the right- and left-skewed shifts, it becomes asymmetric.

Figure 2.2b presents the five CDFs in one graph. The solid curve represents the original normal distribution of income. The dotted one is the location shift, which is parallel and to the right of the solid curve. The dashed curve represents a scale shift, which is no longer parallel to the solid one; the upper half moves farther rightward than the lower half. The upper half of the right-skewed shift curve (long-dash) moves even farther rightward, whereas its bottom tail remains close to that of the original. The left-skewed shift curve (short-dash) moves leftward with the upper half moving farther

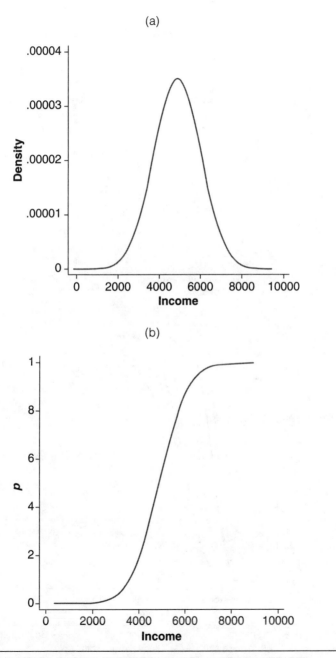

Figure 2.1 PDF and CDF of a Hypothetical Normal Distribution of Income: (a) PDF and (b) CDF

8

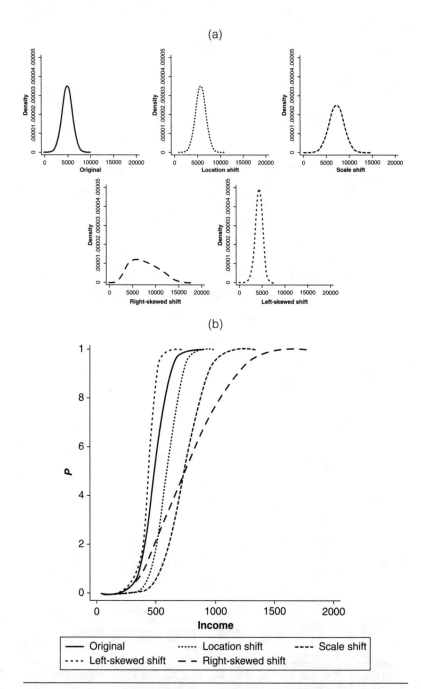

Figure 2.2 Hypothetical Normal Distribution of Income and Its Four Shifted Distributions: (a) PDF and (b) CDF

and the bottom half remaining close to that of the original. While the CDF after the location and scale shifts maintains symmetry, the CDF after the right- and left-skewed shifts does not. Compared with those of the PDFs, patterns for the CDF have different visual representations. Familiarity with the CDF's patterns prepares us to relate the more familiar PDFs to the less familiar quantile function.

Properties of PDFs can be described numerically using moments. Each moment is an expected value of a power of Y, that is, the kth moment is defined as $E[Y^k]$, the first moment is the *mean* (or *expected value*) $\mu = E[Y]$, which is used to describe the central tendency of a distribution. Higher moments ($k = 2, 3, \ldots$) describe more complex properties of a distribution, and are usually easier to understand and interpret when centered at the mean; that is, we consider *central* moments. The kth central moment $E[(Y - \mu)^k]$ is defined as the expected value of the kth power of the difference between Y and μ. In particular, the second central moment (the *variance*) $\sigma^2 = E[(Y - \mu)^2]$, the mean squared difference between Y and μ, measures dispersion (scale). The square root of the variance σ is referred to as the standard deviation of the distribution.

Comparison of higher central moments may be difficult for distributions having different scales, so it is typical to normalize a distribution so that its variance is 1, and then calculate higher-order central moments for the rescaled distribution. The resulting kth normalized central moment is then obtained by dividing the kth central moment by σ^k, so that it takes the form $E[(Y - \mu)^k]/\sigma^K$. In particular, the third normalized central moment takes the form $E[(Y - \mu)^3]/\sigma^3$, a quantity referred to as *skewness*. When the distribution is symmetric about the mean, the skewness takes the value 0. A negative value indicates left skewness, and a positive value indicates right skewness.

Similarly, the fourth central moment gives rise to the quantity $E[(Y - \mu)^4]/\sigma^4$, which is called the *kurtosis* or *peakedness* of a distribution. For the Gaussian (normal) distribution, the kurtosis is 3. A distribution with a higher peak than the Gaussian distribution, if its kurtosis is greater than 3, is termed *leptokurtic*[1]; *platykurtic* when the kurtosis is less than 3. Higher-order moments are less commonly used in describing distributional properties.

A linear transformation of the variable can result in changes in the first and second moments (the mean and variance).[2] If Y has mean μ and variance σ^2 then the mean and variance of $Y^* = a + cY$ are $a + c\mu$ and $c^2\sigma^2$, respectively. On the other hand, because of centering and normalization, the normalized central moments (e.g., skewness and kurtosis) are unaffected by linear transformations.

---

[1]Some people subtract 3 from kurtosis so that the values are distributed around 0.
[2]If Y is a random variable and a and c are constants, then the random variable $Y^* = a + cY$ is referred to as a linear transformation of Y.

Row 1 of Table 2.1 lists the four moments for the generated income data (y_i^0). The mean is \$49,051, the standard deviation is \$10,156, the skewness is 0, and the kurtosis is 3. Rows 2 to 5 show the moments for the probability distribution after each of the four shifts—location, scale, right-skewed, and left-skewed. The location shift caused by adding \$10,000 to everyone's income increases the mean by \$10,000 but does not change the standard deviation, skewness, or kurtosis of the original distribution. The scale shift caused by increasing everyone's income by 50% increases both the mean and the standard deviation; however, it changes neither the skewness nor the kurtosis. The location shift and scale shift are linear transformations of the original variable and thus do not affect the skewness and kurtosis. The right-skewed shift caused by a progressive percentage increase changes all four moments of the original distribution—greater mean, standard deviation, skewness, and smaller kurtosis, opposite for a left-skewed shift.

The last column of Table 2.1 compares the Gini coefficients, with a higher value indicating greater inequality. While the Gini coefficient is to be introduced in the next chapter, the purpose of comparing them here is to show that a location shift and a skewness shift are reflected in a change in the Gini coefficient but a scale shift is not (hence Gini is "scale invariant," see Chapter 4).

Quantile Functions

The quantile function is another tool used to measure inequality, as seen in Pen's (1973) "Parade of Dwarfs" mentioned at the beginning of the chapter. The inverse function of the CDF of income, F_Y, is the quantile function Q_Y,

Distribution	Mean	SD	Skewness	Kurtosis	Gini
Original	49,051	10,156	0.00	3.00	.1167
Location shift	59,051	10,156	0.00	3.00	.0969
Scale shift	73,576	15,233	0.00	3.00	.1167
Right-skew shift	76,441	29,399	0.36	2.40	.2193
Left-skew shift	43,573	6,431	−0.45	4.30	.0807

Table 2.1 Moments and Gini Coefficients of a Hypothetical Normal Distribution of Income and Its Four Shifted Distributions

and $Q_Y^{(p)}$ indicates the value of y such that $F_Y(y) = p$, for each possible proportion p between 0 and 1.

$$Q_Y^{(p)} = F_Y^{-1}(p). \qquad (2.1)$$

Thus, the proportion of the population with values below $Q_Y^{(p)}$ is p (see *Quantile Regression*, Hao & Naiman, 2007, for a more detailed definition).

The graphical representations of the central location, scale, and shape by quantile functions can be seen in Figure 2.3a for the hypothetical normally distributed income data $y_i^{(0)}$. The quantile function's x- and y-axes reverse those of the CDF. Thus, instead of asking for the cumulative probability p at a particular y value, we ask what is the y value at a particular p. Cumulative probability values of interest include $p50$ (the median), $p25$, $p50$, $p75$ (quartiles), $p20$, $p40$, $p60$, $p80$ (quintiles), and $p1, \ldots, p99$ (percentiles). The refocus on quantiles corresponding to given cumulative probabilities facilitates using income as the dependent variable in model-based inequality analyses. The symmetry of quantile functions for a normal distribution mimics the rotation symmetry of their CDF; that is, the slopes on the lower half exactly mirror those on the upper half of the quantile function. A normal distribution exhibits a symmetric curve like the one in Figure 2.3a.

Quantile-based measures provide additional ways to measure the central location, scale, and shape to describe distributional properties. Well-known quantile-based measures include the median ($p50$), which captures the central location, and the interquartile range between $p25$ and $p75$, which captures the scale or dispersion. Extensions to different ranges are flexible, for example, the range between $p10$ and $p90$ or between $p1$ and $p99$. The ratio of the $p50$ to $p90$ range to the $p10$ to $p50$ range captures skewness. Because it is problematic to use the mean and variance to characterize both the central tendency and the dispersion of a distribution that is neither normal nor symmetric, the quantile-based measures offer a much richer solution than using moments to describe distributional properties (see more detailed discussion in *Quantile Regression*, Hao & Naiman, 2007). Quantile-based measures for inequality can be widely applied. It is a common practice to use the median instead of the mean to describe the central tendency for income distribution. Researchers studying income inequality have long been aware that it is inappropriate to use standard deviation to characterize the scale of skewed income distribution. Instead, the natural logarithm of income is often used to change the skewed distribution to a log-normal distribution (e.g., Buchinsky, 1994; Juhn et al., 1993).

Quantile functions can clearly characterize the four shifts from the original normal distribution of income. In Figure 2.3b, the solid curve

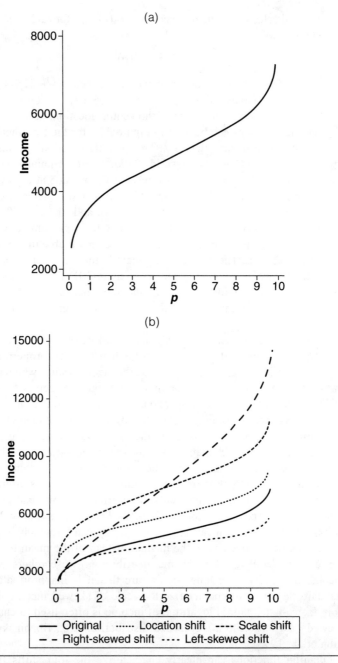

Figure 2.3 Quantile Functions of a Hypothetical Normal Distribution of Income and Its Four Shifted Distributions: (a) Normal and (b) Four Shifts

represents the original distribution. A location shift caused by adding $10,000 to each person's income moves the curve up (the dotted curve), maintaining the symmetry. A scale shift achieved by giving each individual the same percentage raise tilts the curve (the dashed curve), which also maintains the symmetry. Symmetry is lost after the right-skewed shift (the long-dash curve), with its steeper slopes on the upper tail than the lower tail, and also after a left-skewed shift (the short-dash curve), with its flatter slopes on the upper tail than on the lower tail.

Lorenz Curves

The Lorenz curve, introduced in Lorenz (1905), provides a common basis for the Gini coefficient and other scale-invariant scalar inequality measures. It shows, for each possible p between 0 and 1, the proportion of total income that is attributed to those individuals whose income is not higher than the pth quantile. For example, for $p = .25$, we add up all income values at or below $p25$ and express its proportion of the total income.

The most intuitive calculation of the Lorenz curve can be shown with a sample of n incomes $y_1, \ldots, y_n$ by first ranking them to $y_{(1)}, \ldots, y_{(n)}$ and then taking

$$L(s/n) = L(p) = \frac{\sum_{i=1}^{s} y_{(i)}}{\sum_{i=1}^{n} y_i} \text{ for } s = 0, 1, 2, \ldots, n; \ p = s/n. \quad (2.2)$$

Thus, for example, if a sample consists of 100 individuals, and their income is sorted from smallest to largest; we then define $L(.25)$ to be the total income of the lowest 25 individuals, divided by the total income of the population.[3] The Lorenz curve is bounded from below by 0 (when $s = 0$) and from above by 1 (when $s = n$).

The Lorenz curve for the generated income $y_i^{(0)}$ is shown in Figure 2.4a. The x-axis indicates the cumulative proportion of population, and the y-axis indicates the cumulative proportion of total income possessed by the corresponding cumulative proportion of the population. The diagonal straight line, called the *line of equality*, indicates what would result if each person had the exact same share of income. Any departure from equality leads to a Lorenz curve lying below the equality line. Greater deviation of the Lorenz curve from the equality line is indicative of a greater degree of inequality.

The Lorenz curve is closely related to the quantile function and can be expressed using the quantile function. For a population whose

---

[3]Here, y_i is assumed to be nonnegative.

14

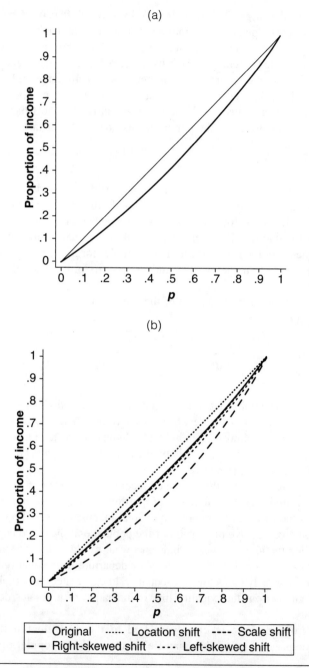

Figure 2.4 Lorenz Curves of a Hypothetical Normal Distribution of Income and Its Four Shifted Distributions: (a) Normal and (b) Four Shifts

distribution has a PDF denoted by f, we have the Lorenz curve as a function of quantiles:

$$L(p) = \frac{\int_{q=0}^{p} Q(q)dq}{\int_{q=0}^{1} Q(q)dq} = \frac{1}{\mu}\int_{y=0}^{Q(p)} yf(y)dy. \qquad (2.3)$$

Graphically, Equation 2.3 can be interpreted to mean that an income share at the Lorenz curve, $L(p)$, corresponding to p in Figure 2.4a is the area under the quantile function curve up to p in Figure 2.3a, normalized by the total area under the quantile function, which is the mean. For example, as shown in the Lorenz curve in Figure 2.4a, about 40% of total income is possessed by the lower half of the population. This cumulative proportion of .4 equals the area under the quantile function up to $p = .5$, normalized by the area under the entire quantile function.

We now consider the effects of a location shift, a scale shift, and a shape shift on the Lorenz curve. For a positive location shift by a ($a > 0$), the new Lorenz curve differs from the original one:

$$L^*(s/n) = \frac{\sum_{i=1}^{s}(a + y_{(i)})}{\sum_{i=1}^{n}(a + y_i)} = \frac{a \cdot s + \sum_{i=1}^{s} y_{(i)}}{a \cdot n + \sum_{i=1}^{n} y_i}. \qquad (2.4)$$

This new Lorenz curve lies above the old one, that is, $L^*(s/n) > L(s/n)$, as long as some incomes are different. Intuitively, a positive location shift increases the numerator disproportionately more than the denominator, thereby moving the Lorenz curve up, whereas a negative location shift decreases the numerator disproportionately more than the denominator, thereby moving the curve down. A rigorous treatment of this fact is given in the appendix to this chapter. Thus, increasing each individual's income by the same positive amount a has the effect of decreasing inequality. In the extreme, as a tends to infinity, the Lorenz curve approaches the equality line. In Figure 2.4b, the positive location shift moves the original Lorenz curve (the solid curve) up slightly, closer to the equality line (the dotted curve).

For a scale shift by c ($c > 0$), we have

$$L^*(s/n) = \frac{\sum_{i=1}^{s} c \cdot y_{(i)}}{\sum_{i=1}^{n} c \cdot y_i} = \frac{c\sum_{i=1}^{s} y_{(i)}}{c\sum_{i=1}^{n} y_i} = L(s/n). \qquad (2.5)$$

Normalized by the mean, the Lorenz curve is invariant to scale shifts (a scale-invariant principle discussed in Chapter 4). Figure 2.4b shows that the original and scale-shift Lorenz curves are identical. In contrast, a scale shift is detected in the PDF, CDF, moments, and quantile function, as shown in previous sections.

The Lorenz curve captures shape shifts. In Figure 2.4b, the right-skewed shift (the rich become richer) moves the Lorenz curve down to the long-dash curve, farther away from the equality line. The left-skewed shift (the rich are taxed more than the poor) moves the Lorenz curve up to the short-dash curve, closer to the equality line.

Generalized Lorenz curves were developed to capture scale shifts (Shorrocks, 1980). Let the *y*-axis now indicate the product of the cumulative share and the mean income. Using our hypothetical data, we show the generalized Lorenz curves for the original normal distribution and its scale shift by increasing everyone's income by 50% in Figure 2.5. The mean income is $49,051 for the original distribution and $73,576 for its scale-shift distribution. Unlike the ordinary Lorenz curves that are identical for these two distributions, the generalized Lorenz curve for the positive scale-shift distribution is *above* that for the original distribution. Furthermore, the two generalized Lorenz curves in Figure 2.5 show that the scale-shifted population is better off than the original population.

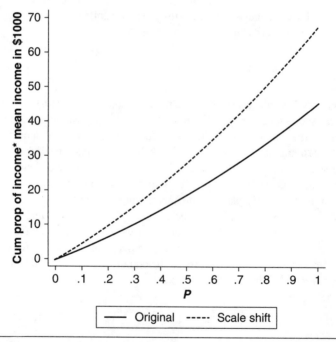

Figure 2.5 Generalized Lorenz Curves of a Hypothetical Normal Distribution of Income and Its Scale Shift

Summary

This chapter briefly introduces four basic tools for measuring and analyzing inequality. It starts from the most elementary tool of the PDF for the attribute under study. Many researchers examine the shape of the probability distribution of the attribute as their first step of empirical work. Central moments of a probability distribution—the mean, variance, skewness, and kurtosis—characterize the central location, scale, and shape of the distribution, which are also widely used by researchers. A second tool, the CDF expresses the area under the PDF. The inverse function of the CDF is the quantile function, our third tool. Finally, the fourth tool—the Lorenz curve—is introduced as a natural extension of the quantile function, because the Lorenz curve expresses the normalized area under the quantile function. Generalized Lorenz curves are introduced to address the scale invariance of ordinary Lorenz curves.

Central to this chapter's sketch of the four basic tools for inequality research are location, scale, and shape shifts, through which we establish the interrelationship among the four basic tools discussed here. This interrelationship will allow us to connect and compare various summary inequality measures, which we introduce in the next chapter.

Appendix: A Location Shift Changes the Lorenz Curve

This appendix provides a proof that a location shift changes the Lorenz curve. There is a misconception that summary inequality measures capture only the dispersion or shape of a distribution, and thus when we compare two distributions, only a change in the dispersion or shape matters. As the Lorenz curve is a common basis that unites many inequality measures, we think this proof is necessary for bettering our understanding of inequality measures.

Observe that as long as some inequality exists, the average income of the lowest s earners is less than the average income of all of the earners. Thus,

$$n \sum_{i=1}^{s} y_{(i)} < s \sum_{i=1}^{n} y_{(i)},$$

which implies

$$an \sum_{i=1}^{s} y_{(i)} < as \sum_{i=1}^{n} y_{(i)}.$$

Finally, adding $\sum_{i=1}^{s} y_{(i)} \sum_{i=1}^{n} y_{(i)}$ to both sides and factoring gives

$$\left(an + \sum_{i=1}^{n} y_{(i)} \right) \sum_{i=1}^{s} y_{(i)} < \left(as + \sum_{i=1}^{s} y_{(i)} \right) \sum_{i=1}^{n} y_{(i)}$$

and hence

$$L^*(s/n) = \frac{\sum_{i=1}^{s} a + y_{(i)}}{\sum_{i=1}^{n} a + y_{(i)}} > \frac{\sum_{i=1}^{s} y_{(i)}}{\sum_{i=1}^{n} y_i} = L(s/n).$$

CHAPTER 3. SUMMARY INEQUALITY MEASURES

This chapter introduces a set of summary inequality measures for continuous, nonnegative measures of resources or well-being, drawn from the large body of inequality literature, particularly from Cowell (2000). We select measures that are widely used, such as the coefficient of variation, the Gini coefficient, and the Theil index, as well as measures that are less commonly used, such as quantile-based measures, the Atkinson family of indexes, and the family of generalized entropy indexes. We illustrate each measure using hypothetical examples used in Chapter 2 to illuminate the analytic aspects of a change in an inequality measure in terms of location, scale, and shape shifts. We then show that changes in inequality in the real world over time has a combination of explanations, using the 1991 and 2001 data from the Survey of Income and Program Participation (SIPP), which is also used in *Quantile Regression*, the first of the two-book series. We use the package "inequal7" in Stata to obtain various summary inequality measures (Van Kerm, 2001).

Summary Inequality Measures

The measures we consider are chosen either because they are commonly used in empirical work or because they possess specific strengths. We organize our review by relating summary inequality measures to underlying probability distributions and their quantile functions, Lorenz curves, social welfare functions, and information theory.

Relating Inequality Measures to Probability Distributions

The simplest measure of income inequality is obtained directly from the ordered individual incomes. The spread of income can be expressed as the distance from the minimum income to the maximum income, the *range R*:

$$R = y_{\max} - y_{\min}. \tag{3.1}$$

If we know the income of the whole population, the range effectively captures the entire spread of the distribution. Row 1 of Table 3.1 shows the range for the hypothetical symmetric distribution of income and its four shifted distributions. The range for the original distribution is $86,000. The pure location shift does not change the original range. The scale shift and the right-skewed shift both increase the spread, while the left-skewed shift reduces it as shown in Table 3.1. Using the real-world data from the SIPP, Row 1 of Table 3.2 shows that the income range was $467,000 in 1991 and

19

grew to $728,000 in 2001, reflecting the changes in the scale and shape of the U.S. income distribution.

The range, however, is very sensitive to incomplete information on the response for everyone in a population and, it may be excessively influenced by a few extreme values. On the other hand, confidentiality reasons make top-coding income a common practice, which effectively masks the income range. A more popular dispersion measure is the second central moment of the distribution, the *variance V*:

$$V = \frac{1}{n}\sum_{i=1}^{n}(y_i - \bar{y})^2. \tag{3.2}$$

The variance of income will increase if everyone gets a fixed percentage raise. For example, a fixed 50% increase in each person's income would lead to an increase in variance by a factor of $1.50^2 = 2.25$,[1] while maintaining the same shape of the income distribution. Row 2 of Table 3.1 shows that the standard deviation (the square root of variance) for the 1.5-scale shift is 1.5 times of that of the original distribution. The right-skewed shift increases the standard deviation by nearly three times, whereas the left-skewed shift decreases it by about 40%. Row 2 of Table 3.2 shows that the standard deviation of income increased from 35.8 thousand dollars in 1991 to 45.3 thousand dollars in 2001.

If we wish to compare income distributions without being influenced by income magnitudes, we can divide the standard deviation (the square root of the variance) by the mean, to give *coefficient of variation c*:

$$c = \frac{\sqrt{V}}{\bar{y}}. \tag{3.3}$$

This measure is insensitive to a fixed percentage change in income, a property termed *scale invariance*.[2] The third row of Table 3.1 shows that c remains 0.207 for the original and scale-shift distributions. However, it decreases after a pure positive location shift (0.172) and a left-skewed shift (0.148), whereas it increases after a right-skewed shift (0.385). Thus, the coefficient of variation captures location and skewness shifts but not scale shifts. The increase from 0.738 to 0.900 from 1991 to 2001 in Row 3 of Table 3.2 indicates an increase in central location as well as the right skewness of the U.S. income distribution.

---

[1]To see this, we have the following: $\frac{1}{n}\sum_{i=1}^{n}(1.5y_i - 1.5\bar{y})^2 = 1.5^2 \cdot \frac{1}{n}\sum_{i=1}^{n}(y_i - \bar{y})^2 = 1.5^2 V.$

[2]Using the 50% raise example, we have the following:

$$c = \frac{\sqrt{\frac{1}{n}\sum_{i=1}^{n}(1.5y_i - 1.5\bar{y})^2}}{1.5\bar{y}} = \frac{\sqrt{\frac{1}{n}\sum_{i=1}^{n}(y_i - \bar{y})^2}}{\bar{y}} = \frac{\sqrt{V}}{\bar{y}}.$$

	Inequality Measures	Original	Location Shift	Scale Shift	Right-Skewed Shift	Left-Skewed Shift
	Related to the probability distribution					
1	R (range) in $1,000	86	86	128	175	68
2	$\sqrt{V}$ (standard deviation) in $1,000	10.1	10.1	15.2	29.4	6.4
3	c (coefficient of variation)	0.207	0.172	0.207	0.385	0.148
4	v (logarithmic variance)	0.049	0.032	0.049	0.178	0.026
5	v_1 (variance of the logarithms)	0.049	0.032	0.049	0.172	0.026
	Based on quantile functions and Lorenz curves					
6	$p5/p50$ (quantile ratio)	0.662	0.720	0.662	0.464	0.728
7	$p95/p50$ (quantile ratio)	1.343	1.284	1.343	1.745	1.208
8	Share of bottom fifth	0.142	0.152	0.142	0.1010	0.1566
9	Share of top fifth	0.258	0.248	0.258	0.315	0.238
10	G (Gini coefficient)	0.117	0.097	0.117	0.219	0.081

(Continued)

	Inequality Measures	Original	Location Shift	Scale Shift	Right-Skewed Shift	Left-Skewed Shift
	Derived from social welfare functions					
11	$A_{1/2}$ (Atkinson's index, $\varepsilon = 1/2$)	0.011	0.007	0.011	0.038	0.006
12	A_1 (Atkinson's index, $\varepsilon = 1$)	0.023	0.015	0.023	0.077	0.012
13	A_2 (Atkinson's index, $\varepsilon = 2$)	0.048	0.032	0.048	0.158	0.026
	Developed from information theory					
14	T (Theil index) GE_1 (generalized entropy $\theta = 1$)	0.022	0.015	0.022	0.075	0.011
15	GE_0 (generalized entropy $\theta = 0$)	0.023	0.016	0.023	0.080	0.012
16	GE_{-1} (generalized entropy $\theta = -1$)	0.025	0.016	0.025	0.094	0.013
17	GE_2 (generalized entropy $\theta = 2$)	0.021	0.015	0.021	0.074	0.011

Table 3.1 Inequality Measures for Five Hypothetical Income Distributions

	Inequality Measures	1991	2001
	Related to the probability distribution		
1	R (range) in $1,000	467	728
2	$\sqrt{V}$ (standard deviation) in $1,000	35.8	45.3
3	c (coefficient of variation)	0.738	0.900
4	v (logarithmic variance)	0.790	0.969
5	v_1 (variance of the logarithms)	0.707	0.846
	Based on quantile functions and Lorenz curves		
6	$p5/p50$ (quantile ratio)	0.194	0.190
7	$p95/p50$ (quantile ratio)	2.866	3.232
8	Share of bottom fifth	0.048	0.043
9	Share of top fifth	0.430	0.466
10	G (Gini coefficient)	0.385	0.424
	Derived from social welfare functions		
11	$A_{1/2}$ (Atkinson's index, $\varepsilon = 1/2$)	0.123	0.149
12	A_1 (Atkinson's index, $\varepsilon = 1$)	0.251	0.294
13	A_2 (Atkinson's index, $\varepsilon = 2$)	0.734	0.875
	Developed from information theory		
14	T (Theil index) GE_1 (generalized entropy $\theta = 1$)	0.244	0.310
15	GE_0 (generalized entropy $\theta = 0$)	0.288	0.349
16	GE_{-1} (generalized entropy $\theta = -1$)	1.378	3.512
17	GE_2 (generalized entropy $\theta = 2$)	0.272	0.405

Table 3.2   Inequality Measures for Household Income: SIPP 1991 and 2001

Note: SIPP, Survey of Income and Program Participation.

In addition to variance, we can measure inequality using the *logarithmic variance*

$$\nu = \frac{1}{n}\sum_{i=1}^{n}\left(\log\left(\frac{y_i}{\bar{y}}\right)\right)^2 = \frac{1}{n}\sum_{i=1}^{n}\left(\log y_i - \log \bar{y}\right)^2. \qquad (3.4)$$

Such a measure can be useful to reduce the spread of a heavily right-skewed distribution due to a log transformation of the data. The term *variance* is misleading because in Expression 3.4, the average of squared deviations is not about the mean of the log-transformed data $\overline{\log(y)}$, but rather, about the log of the mean, $\log(\bar{y})$. Still, this measure has the scale invariance property. A 50% raise in income for everyone has no effect on the quantity ν.

For the reason mentioned above, it is statistically more natural to define the *variance of the logarithms* ν_1, that is, we compute the variance of the log-transformed data.[3] This measure takes a form similar to the logarithmic variance, except that it replaces the arithmetic mean $\bar{y}$ with the geometric mean y^*:

$$\nu_1 = \frac{1}{n}\sum_{i=1}^{n}\left(\log\left(\frac{y_i}{y^*}\right)\right)^2 = \frac{1}{n}\sum_{i=1}^{n}\left(\log(y_i) - \overline{\log(y)}\right)^2. \qquad (3.5)$$

The scale invariance property is then straightforward to see. If we replace each y_i with cy_i, then $\log(cy_i) = \log(c) + \log(y_i)$, and $\overline{\log(cy)} = \log(c) + \overline{\log(y)}$, hence

$$\frac{1}{n}\sum_{i=1}^{n}\left(\log(cy_i) - \overline{\log(cy)}\right)^2 = \frac{1}{n}\sum_{i=1}^{n}\left(\log(c) + \log(y_i) - \log(c) - \overline{\log(y)}\right)^2,$$

so we can cancel the $\log(c)$ terms and recover the original ν_1. Consequently, a fixed percentage raise in income for the whole population does not affect the value of the variance of the logarithms. Both ν and ν_1 are scale invariant and the proper choice between them depends on whether the functional transformation (here lognormal) is important in a particular study. However, we prefer ν_1 for the reason mentioned above.

The logarithmic variance ν for the symmetric distribution of income and its four shifted distributions are shown in Row 4 of Table 3.1. It is 0.049 for the symmetric income and is unaltered after the scale shift. The positive

---

[3]The geometric mean is defined as $\left(\prod_{i=1}^{n} y_i\right)^{\frac{1}{n}}$, which is equivalent to $e^{\frac{1}{n}\sum_{i=1}^{n}\log y_i}$ for $y_i > 0$.
The geometric mean is always less than or equal to the arithmetic mean. The log of geometric mean of income is the mean of the log income.

location shift effectively increases the ratio of $y_i/\bar{y}$ for incomes below the mean and decreases the ratio for incomes above the mean, thereby decreasing the value of v to 0.032. The left-skewed shift also changes the ratio of $y_i/\bar{y}$ in a similar but more intense manner, reducing v to 0.026. In contrast, the right-skewed shift changes the ratio of $y_i/\bar{y}$ in the opposite direction, raising v to 0.178. The American household income became more unequal with a logarithmic variance increase from 0.790 to 0.969 due to both location and shape shifts (see Row 4 of Table 3.2).

Row 5 of Tables 3.1 and 3.2 shows that while the variance of the logarithms v_1 largely resembles the logarithmic variance v, v is usually slightly greater than v_1, and the difference becomes larger when the distribution is more right or left skewed.

Inequality Measures Based on Quantile Functions and Lorenz Curves

Quantiles of the income distribution are often used in government statistics and the economic analysis of income inequality. For instance, the contrast between the bottom fifth and the top fifth of the income distribution directly shows uneven income distribution. Changes in quantile ratios of noncentral quantiles to the median are often used to show the trend of shape shifts of income distribution or wealth distribution.

A bottom-sensitive quantile ratio is $p5/p50$, while a top-sensitive quantile ratio is $p95/p50$. Rows 6 and 7 in Table 3.1 show that quantile ratios remain unchanged after a scale shift but are sensitive to location shift, right-skewed shift, and left skewed shift. For example, a positive location shift reduces inequality as the $p5/p50$ increases, while the $p95/p50$ decreases. Rows 6 and 7 in Table 3.2 show that the $p5/p50$ ratio is virtually unchanged between 1991 (0.194) and 2001 (0.190), whereas the $p95/p50$ increases considerably from 2.866 to 3.232. These results suggest the stagnation of the lower end and the expansion of the upper end of the U.S. income distribution.

Quantile-based inequality measures are flexible. Researchers can decide which quantiles are most meaningful, depending on the subject matter. For example, if we want to know the time trend of income distribution with a focus on the middle class, we can choose $p25$ and $p75$. Another example is educational achievement trends; educational experts often define achievement categories based on standardized test scores. According to the National Assessment of Educational Progress in 2000, the basic achievement level for the eighth graders' science test score is 143 points, which is the 39th percentile ($p39$) of the nation's science test score distribution. The proficiency level (170 points) and the advanced level (208 points) are the 69th percentile ($p69$) and the 97th percentile ($p97$) of the test score distribution, respectively. Using these particular choices of quantiles over time provides a logical way to monitor achievement trends rather than using arbitrary quantiles. At the same time, this flexibility means that we lack a unique quantile-based measure.

Official statistics regarding income inequality use the notion of an income *share*. For example, the U.S. Census Bureau reported that the top 1% of wage earners hold 23% of total income in 2007, the highest inequality level since 1913. An income share is a proportion of total income that is attributed to the individuals/households whose income is in some particular quantile range. For example, we may ask, "What proportion of total population income corresponds to the top 10% of moneymakers?"

For the Lorenz curve,

$$L(s/n) = \frac{\sum_{i=1}^{s} y_{(i)}}{\sum_{i=1}^{n} y_i}$$

is the proportion of income attributed to the s individuals having the lowest incomes. Thus, the Lorenz curve at a point p ($p = s/n$) gives the share attributed to the bottom $100p\%$ of individuals/households directly (as $L(p)$). The Lorenz curve can also be used, less directly, to arrive at a top share. Observe that proportion of income attributed to the s individuals with the highest incomes can be written as

$$\frac{\sum_{i=n-s+1}^{n} y_{(i)}}{\sum_{i=1}^{n} y_{(i)}} = \frac{\sum_{i=1}^{n} y_{(i)} - \sum_{i=1}^{n-s} y_{(i)}}{\sum_{i=1}^{n} y_{(i)}} = 1 - \frac{\sum_{i=1}^{n-s} y_{(i)}}{\sum_{i=1}^{n} y_{(i)}},$$

which is $1 - L((n - s)/n) = 1 - L(1 - (s/n))$. Thus, generally speaking, the share of the top $100p\%$ of individuals/households is given by $1 - L(1 - p)$.

To get a middle share, that is, the proportion of total income that corresponds to the individuals whose income is between two percentiles, say the $100p_L\%$ and $100p_U\%$ of individuals, we take the difference between the upper share and the lower share $L(p_U) - L(p_L)$.

Rows 8 and 9 in Table 3.1 show the bottom and top fifth shares for the five distributions. Observing how the income share for the bottom fifth is considerably smaller than the income share for the top fifth provides an intuitive way of feeling for degrees of inequality. Over the 10 years from 1991 to 2001, the income share of the bottom quintile stagnated from 0.048 to 0.043, while the income share of the top fifth increased from 0.43 to 0.47 (see Rows 8 and 9 in Table 3.2). The Lorenz curve can be used to inspect a variety of quantiles (not only quintiles) to measure inequality. Both quantile ratios and share measures possess the scale invariance property.

Changes in Lorenz curves over time do not always convey a clear pattern about the change in inequality over time. When the Lorenz curves for two periods intersect, we cannot conclude which period is more unequal than the other. We will provide a more detailed discussion about the intersection of Lorenz curves in Chapter 5.

The flexibility of quantile-based and share-based inequality measures is appealing to many researchers and audiences. Still, this flexibility comes with a price in that the amount of the summary data can become over-whelming. It is up to the researchers to choose among a set of flexible measures or one summary measure for the whole income distribution, according to the particular research context.

The *Gini coefficient* G can be defined directly from the Lorenz curve and has a simple graphical interpretation. Since the Lorenz curve in the complete equality case is represented by the diagonal, and the Lorenz curve always lies on or below the diagonal, we can measure the distance from complete equality by computing the area below the diagonal and above the Lorenz curve. The difference in the two areas is multiplied by a factor two to give an inequality measure that ranges between zero and one. Larger values of the Gini coefficient correspond to greater levels of inequality.

Figure 3.1 presents four different Lorenz curves for the minimum, maximum, and two other values of Gini coefficient G. Figure 3.1a cor-responds to the case of complete equality, $G = 0$, when every individual receives an equal share of the total income. Situations b and c in Figure 3.1 correspond to instances in which some individuals have more income than others, with Situation b being less unequal than Situation c. The most extreme case of inequality, when one person possesses all the income and the $n - 1$ persons have no income at all, is represented by a Lorenz curve shown in Figure 3.1d, with the area measured for the Gini coefficient being the entire lower-right triangular half of the unit square, leading to $G = 1$.

Various equivalent formulas are available for calculating the Gini coef-ficient. Letting $L(p)$ denote the Lorenz function evaluated at a particular proportion p, we can express the area between the equality curve and the Lorenz curve as the difference between the area A below the equality line and the area B below the Lorenz curve. Hence, one way to express the Gini coefficient is to write the following:

$$G = 2(A - B) = 2\left(\int_0^1 p\,dp - \int_0^1 L(p)dp\right) = 2\int_0^1 [(p - L(p)]dp. \quad (3.6a)$$

On the other hand, a formula for the Gini coefficient in terms of income differences of all possible pairs in the population $y_1, \ldots, y_n$ is available,

28

(a)

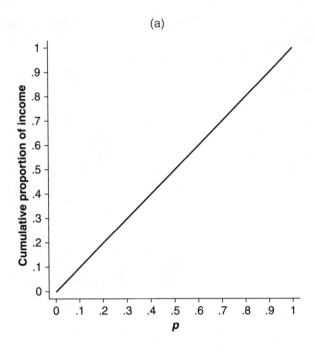

(b)

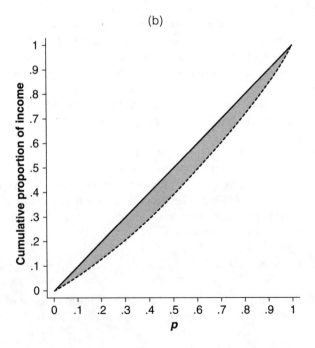

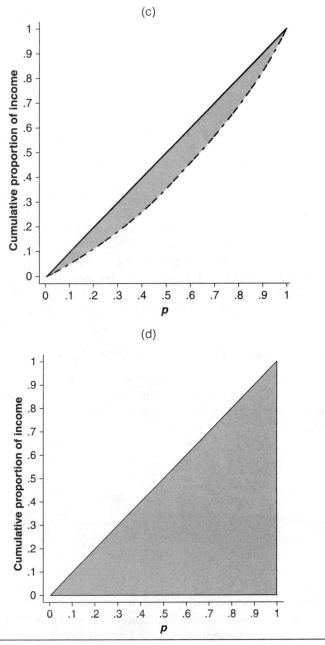

Figure 3.1 Lorenz Curves for the Minimum, Maximum, and Two Other Values of Gini

namely, half of the average difference between all $n(n - 1)/2$ possible pairs of population incomes, normalized by the mean income:

$$G = \frac{1}{2} \frac{\sum\limits_{1 \leq j < i \leq n}^{n} |y_i - y_j| / (n(n-1)/2)}{\bar{y}} = \frac{\sum\limits_{1 \leq j < i \leq n}^{n} |y_i - y_j|}{n(n-1)\bar{y}}. \qquad (3.6b)$$

This formula shows clearly that the minimum of the Gini coefficient is 0 when everyone has an equal share of the total income (Figure 3.1a). In addition, the maximum of 1 is obtained when one person has the total income (Figure 3.1d) so that the range of G is [0,1] (Figure 3.1b and c).

Row 10 of Table 3.1 shows that the Gini coefficient G for the symmetric distribution of income is 0.117. The G declines under a pure location shift in Column 2 (0.097). The G is scale invariant because it is based on the Lorenz curve, which is itself scale invariant, as noted in Chapter 2. The scale invariance is also clear from Equation 3.6b, because the mean income $\bar{y}$ appears in the denominator. The left-skewed shift reduces the G to 0.081, while the right-skewed shift raises G to 0.219. The G for the U.S. income increased from 0.385 in 1991 to 0.424 in 2001, reflecting both location and shape shifts (although not a scale shift).

Inequality Measures Derived From Social Welfare Functions

In this section, we describe how inequality measures can be obtained using *social welfare functions*. Following Atkinson (1970), the income components for a society consisting of n individuals are combined into an n-tuple $(y_1, \ldots, y_n)$, with y_i representing the income level of the ith individual. A social welfare function is a function that assigns to each possible income n-tuple a value $W(y_1, \ldots, y_n)$, meant to represent the society's collective well-being when that particular income n-tuple is obtained. Thus, if $W(y_1, \ldots, y_n) \geq W(\tilde{y}_1, \ldots, \tilde{y}_n)$, then $(y_1, \ldots, y_n)$ is viewed as more desirable than $(\tilde{y}_1, \ldots, \tilde{y}_n)$ for the society collectively.

Properties of social welfare functions can be used to reflect societal goals of equality and equity (Deaton, 1997). For example, we may impose on a social welfare function a property under which more equal distributions are viewed as preferable to less equal ones, so that holding the total income of a society constant, the social welfare is highest when income is equally distributed. Also, a social welfare function may be structured so that social welfare increases whenever any single individual is made better off, and no one is left worse-off (Pareto improvements), a property referred to as *equity preference*.

For simplicity the social welfare function is assumed to be an aggregate of individual utilities, so it takes a simple additive form $W(y_1, \ldots, y_n) = \sum_{i=1}^{n} U(y_i)$. Here U is a function that is meant to reflect the utility that each individual associated with a particular income level, and is referred to as the *social utility function*. This function is assumed to be the same for all individuals. We will restrict attention to social welfare functions formed in this manner, where U is assumed to be monotone nondecreasing and concave. These assumptions are natural ones: the monotonicity guarantees that the equity preference property holds. The concavity assumption is a common one and amounts to the assumption of diminishing marginal utility.

Under these assumptions, the social welfare function is concave, meaning that the social welfare corresponding to the weighted average of two income n-tuples is at least as great as the weighted average of the social welfare associated with each. It follows that social welfare does not decrease when a simple income transfer is made between a richer person and a poorer person so long as the rank between these two persons remains unchanged. This is the "principle of transfers" originally proposed by Dalton (1920), which will be discussed further in Chapter 4.

Once the specific form of a social welfare function is arrived at, it is possible to introduce inequality measures based on the concept of *equally distributed equivalent income*. This is defined as the income y^* received by every individual that would give rise to the same social welfare as actually obtained, i.e. the solution to $W(y^*, \ldots, y^*) = W(y_1, \ldots, y_n)$, or equivalently, $U(y^*) = \frac{1}{n} \sum_{i=1}^{n} U(y_i)$. The equally distributed equivalent income is invariant under affine transformation of the social utility function, U, meaning that if we define a new social utility function $\tilde{U}$ in terms of a social utility function U by taking $\tilde{U}(y) = aU(y) + b$ for some choice of constants a and b, with $a > 0$, then y^* is the same for both U and $\tilde{U}$.

Under the assumptions mentioned above, we have $W(y^*, \ldots, y^*) \leq W(\bar{y}, \ldots, \bar{y})$, so that $y^* \leq \bar{y}$, that is, the equally distributed income is no greater than the mean income. A proof of this fact may be found in the Chapter 3 Appendix. A posted at the author's web site. By equally distributing all available income, society is better off from the social welfare perspective. The ratio $y^*/\bar{y}$ can then be viewed as a measure of equality. If the ratio is close to one, then society can equally redistribute all of its available income and achieve roughly the same level of social welfare. If the ratio is 40% then society can achieve perfect equality by reducing total income to 40% of its current value and distributing it equally. The less reduction in income required to equi-distribute all income and achieve the same social welfare, the closer society is to equality. Atkinson (1970) introduced the idea of using quantity $1 - y^*/\bar{y}$ to measure inequality. This quantity also takes values between zero and one with zero representing complete equality. Larger values represent greater inequality, but depending on the social utility function, the value one may not be attainable.

The invariance property for y^* under affine transformations of the utility function leads immediately to the same property for the corresponding inequality measures. This is appealing in that adjusting the social utility function by a shift or change in scale should not affect the measure of inequality. One final key property that is natural to impose on our inequality measure is income scale invariance: if we replace the income n-tuple $(y_1, \ldots, y_n)$ by $(cy_1, \ldots, cy_n)$ for a positive constant c, the level of inequality should be unchanged. When we impose this condition on the inequality measure, the possibilities for social utility functions are reduced to the set of affine transformations of social utility functions of the form $U(y) = y^c$, for some value of c less than or equal to one, or $U(y) = \log(y)$. It is customary to use the parameter $\varepsilon = 1 - c$, instead of c, and to express the family of social utility functions using the affine transformed versions $U_\varepsilon(y) = (y^{1-\varepsilon} - 1)/(1 - \varepsilon)$, where ε is constrained to be nonnegative. Note that the case of $\varepsilon = 1$ is not well-defined in the above definition, but this convention enables us to view $U(y) = \log(y)$ as a limiting case in this family, as $\varepsilon \to 1$,[4] so we use the notation $U_1(y)$ for this special case. Note that for $\varepsilon \geq 1$, the value of $U_\varepsilon(0)$ is not well defined, but it is the case that in the limit as y approaches zero, the value of $U_\varepsilon(y)$ approaches $-\infty$, hence society can be viewed as being in an infinitely unhealthy state if any single individual has no income. Since no income for some can be a common occurrence, use of values of ε in this range may prove problematic.

We have arrived at a family of social welfare functions possessing several desirable properties: $W_\varepsilon = \dfrac{1}{n}\sum_{i=1}^{n}\dfrac{y_i^{1-\varepsilon} - 1}{1 - \varepsilon}$ for values of the parameter ε, which is taken to be nonnegative, and where we interpret W_1 as $\dfrac{1}{n}\sum_{i=1}^{n}\log(y_i)$. The parameter ε is referred to as the *inequality aversion parameter,* for reasons that will soon become clear. The choice of this parameter is meant to reflect behavior of society as a whole.

Once the choice of the inequality aversion parameter is determined, it is straightforward to arrive at the equally distributed equivalent income, by

---

[4]Using L'Hôpital's rule we see that $\lim_{\varepsilon \to 1}(y^{1-\varepsilon} - 1)/(1 - \varepsilon) = \dfrac{d}{d\varepsilon}(y^{1-\varepsilon} - 1)/\dfrac{d}{d\varepsilon}(1 - \varepsilon) = \log(y).$

solving the equation $U_\varepsilon(y^*) = \dfrac{1}{n} \sum\limits_{i=1}^{n} U_\varepsilon(y_i)$ and this leads to the solution

$y^* = \left(\dfrac{1}{n} \sum\limits_{i=1}^{n} y_i^{1-\varepsilon} \right)^{1/(1-\varepsilon)}$. It should be emphasized here that each choice of the inequality aversion parameter ε gives rise to a different value of y^*, so to avoid confusion we may use the notation $y^*(\varepsilon)$ for this quantity. When $\varepsilon = 0$ the equally distributed equivalent income is $\bar{y}$, the mean income, which happens to coincide with the social welfare value. Thus, for small values of the inequality aversion parameter, any income inequality that leaves total income unchanged has minimal effect on social welfare. For the special case when ε equals one, we obtain the geometric mean $y^*(1) = \left(\prod\limits_{i=1}^{n} y_i \right)^{1/n}$.

A derivation (see Chapter 3, Appendix A, posted on the authors' Web site) shows that the equally distributed equivalent income $y^*(\varepsilon)$ decreases as the inequality aversion parameter ε increases. In case a single individual's income is zero and $\varepsilon > 1$, the exponent in $y_i^{1-\varepsilon}$ is negative and we can interpret the expression for $y^*(\varepsilon)$ as zero since this is the value attained in the limit if the income vector is viewed as a limit of a sequence of income vectors having all positive components.

At this point we can introduce the Atkinson *family of inequality indices* A_ε, which are the Atkinson measures associated with the specific forms of social utility functions under consideration, for each possible value of $\varepsilon \geq 0$. These are obtained directly from the expressions for the $y^*(\varepsilon)$ and can be written in the form

$$A_\varepsilon(y_1, \ldots, y_n) = 1 - y^*(\varepsilon)/\bar{y} = 1 - \left[\dfrac{1}{n} \sum\limits_{i=1}^{n} \left(\dfrac{y_i}{\bar{y}} \right)^{1-\varepsilon} \right]^{\frac{1}{1-\varepsilon}} \qquad (3.7)$$

when $\varepsilon \neq 1$, and in the special case when $\varepsilon = 1$ we have

$$A_1(y_1, \ldots, y_n) = 1 - \left\{ \prod\limits_{i=1}^{n} (y_i/\bar{y}) \right\}^{1/n}.$$

It now becomes clear why ε can be referred to as the inequality aversion parameter. Inequality, being defined in Atkinson's approach as $1 - y^*(\varepsilon)/\bar{y}$, increases as the parameter ε increases. If ε is very close to zero, the Atkinson index takes a value close to zero no matter how income is distributed, and society may be described as indifferent to income inequality. For two different societies having exactly the same income allocations, with the first society having parameter ε_1 and the second having parameter ε_2, with $\varepsilon_1 < \varepsilon_2$, the second society would judge its inequality to be greater and could be described as more averse to inequality differences.

The range of possible values that can be taken on by the Atkinson index is important to consider. At the lower end, when income is equally distributed throughout the population, $y_i = \bar{y}$ for all i, and all of the Atkinson indices take the value zero. At the upper end, the index can never exceed one. For $\varepsilon < 1$ maximum inequality is attained when one individual has all of the income and we obtain $A_\varepsilon = 1 - n^{-\varepsilon/(1-\varepsilon)}$. This value will be close to one if n is large and ε is not too close to zero. If $\varepsilon \geq 1$ then A_ε can be made as close to one as desired by income vectors with one individual receiving almost all of the income and the remaining population sharing what is left.

Row 11 of Table 3.1 records the values of $A^{1/2}$. It is .011 for the symmetric distribution of income, and it remains the same after the scale shift. The positive location shift effectively increases the ratio of $y_i/\bar{y}$ for incomes below the mean and decreases the ratio for incomes above the mean, thereby decreasing inequality measured by the Atkinson index (0.007). Similarly, the left-skewed shift changes the ratio of $y_i/\bar{y}$, reducing $A^{1/2}$ to 0.006. In contrast, the right-skewed shift changes the ratio of $y_i/\bar{y}$ and raises $A^{1/2}$ to 0.038. Increasing the inequality aversion leads to greater inequality, as shown in Rows 12 and 13 of Table 3.1, where doubling ε from $\varepsilon = 1$ to $\varepsilon = 2$ leads to slightly over twice the inequality. The real-world data from the SIPP in Rows 11 to 13 in Table 3.2 show that $A^{1/2}$ increased from 0.123 in 1991 to 0.149 in 2001. The value of A_2 is almost three times that of A_1 for both years.

Inequality Measures Developed From Information Theory

Entropy

Information theory quantifies the degree of randomness of a probability distribution (or equivalently of a random variable) using a measure referred to as *information entropy* or *Shannon entropy*. The term *entropy* captures uncertainty. If we consider an experiment in which a random variable can take one of n possible values, with probabilities $p_1, \ldots, p_n$, then the entropy associated with the distribution is defined to be

$$H(p_1, \ldots, p_n) = -\sum_{i=1}^{n} p_i \log_2(p_i).$$

Observe that the base of the logarithm used to define the entropy is conveniently taken to be 2. (One can define entropy using any base, which only has the effect of multiplying all entropies by a constant factor; that is, if we use instead the natural logarithm, denoted by log(), then all entropies defined as above are multiplied by log(2).) If some outcome is certain, so that $p_i = 1$ for some i (making all the other probabilities zero), then the entropy is zero.[5]

Perhaps the simplest example to consider is the case of an experiment consisting of a flip of a fair coin. Here, there are two possible outcomes, each having probability 1/2, making the entropy

$$H(1/2, 1/2) = -\frac{1}{2}\log_2(1/2) - \frac{1}{2}\log_2(1/2) = 1.$$

This example explains why the base of the logarithm is taken to be 2. Entropy is viewed as the number of bits required to encode the information in an experiment. Here the result of the experiment, which has two possible outcomes, requires a single bit. One can think of entropy as measuring randomness of a distribution using fair coin tosses as the basic unit. More generally, we can consider a two-outcome experiment where the outcomes have probabilities p and $1 - p$, where p is any number between 0 and 1. Such an experiment is referred to as a Bernoulli trial. Here the entropy is given by

$$H(p, 1 - p) = -p\log_2(p) - (1 - p)\log_2(1 - p) = -\log_2(p^p(1 - p)^{1-p}).$$

The graph of this entropy expression as a function of resembles an inverted parabola that is symmetric about 1/2 and whose maximum occurs at 1/2. Intuitively, for the flip of a biased coin, the entropy (uncertainty) is maximized when the probability of heads is 1/2.

If X is a random variable taking n possible values with probabilities $p_1, \ldots, p_n$, then we can refer to $H(p_1, \ldots, p_n)$ as the entropy of X and denote this by $H(X)$. The entropy only depends on the probabilities of the outcomes in an experiment, and the particular labels given to these outcomes themselves have no bearing whatsoever. As a consequence, the entropy corresponding to an experiment with outcome probabilities $p_1, \ldots, p_n$ is unaffected when the outcomes (and hence the probabilities) are reordered.

Entropy has many important properties, and we record some of them here. One key property is additivity under independence. Consider two experiments: In the first experiment, we observe a random variable X whose entropy is $H(X)$, and in the second experiment, we observe Y with entropy $H(Y)$; then in the combined experiment in which we observe the

---

[5]When $p = 0$ the logarithm of p is undefined, but we can define the limit as $p \to 0$ of $p \log(p)$ is 0 and the function $p \log(p)$ is continuous.

pair (X, Y) with X and Y independent, the entropy for the pair (X, Y) is the sum of the entropies

$$H(X, Y) = H(X) + H(Y).$$

To see this, suppose X takes values $1, \ldots, m$ with probabilities $p_1, \ldots, p_m$, Y takes values $1, \ldots, n$ with probabilities $q_1, \ldots, q_n$, and the pair (X, Y) takes value (i, j) with probability $p_i q_j$. Thus, the entropy corresponding to the combined experiment is given by the following:

$$
\begin{aligned}
H &= -\sum_{i,j} p_i q_j \log(p_i q_j) = -\sum_{i,j} p_i q_j (\log(p_i) + \log(q_j)) \\
&= -\sum_i \sum_j p_i q_j \log(p_i) + -\sum_j \sum_i p_i q_j \log(q_j) \\
&= -\sum_i p_i \log(p_i) \sum_j q_j - \sum_j q_j \log(q_j) \sum_i p_i \\
&= -\sum_i p_i \log(p_i) - \sum_j q_j \log(q_j) = H(X) + H(Y).
\end{aligned}
$$

Since the entropy of a probability distribution is defined no matter how many outcomes there are, we need to understand how entropies relate to one another for different numbers of outcomes. For example, if H is the entropy corresponding to probabilities $p_1, \ldots, p_n$, and one of these probabilities, p_i is broken up into two pieces, say $p_i = q_i + r_i$, then the entropy increases, that is,

$$H(p_1, \ldots, p_{i-1}, q_i + r_i, p_{i+1}, \ldots, P_n) \leq H(p_1, \ldots, p_{i-1}, q_i, r_i, p_{i+1}, \ldots, p_n).$$

In addition, the entropy function is *concave*,[6] so that for a pair of probability distributions $p_1, \ldots, p_n$ and $q_1, \ldots, q_n$ and for a constant $\lambda \in [0,1]$, we have

$$
\begin{aligned}
&H(\lambda(p_1, \ldots, p_n) + (1 - \lambda)(q_1, \ldots, q_n)) \\
&\geq \lambda H(p_1, \ldots, p_n) + (1 - \lambda) H(q_1, \ldots q_n).
\end{aligned}
$$

This inequality has the following interpretation. The distribution with probabilities,

$$
\begin{aligned}
&\lambda(p_1, \ldots, p_n) + (1 - \lambda)(q_1, \ldots, q_n) \\
&= (\lambda p_1 + (1 - \lambda) q_1, \ldots, \lambda p_n + (1 - \lambda) q_n),
\end{aligned}
$$

---

[6]A function $f(x_1, \ldots, x_n)$ of several variables is said to be *concave* if its graph on any line segment connecting a pair of points lies above the graph of the linear interpolation of the function between those two points. Formally, we have $f(\lambda(x_1, \ldots, x_n) + (1 - \lambda)(y_1, \ldots, y_n)) \geq \lambda f(x_1, \ldots, x_n) + (1 - \lambda) f(y_1, \ldots, y_n)$ for all choices of $(x_1, \ldots, x_n)$, $(y_1, \ldots y_n)$, and λ between 0 and 1.

can be thought of as the distribution that results from flipping a biased coin and sampling from the distribution defined by $p_1, \ldots, p_n$ with probability λ and from the distribution defined by $q_1, \ldots, q_n$ with probability $1 - \lambda$. This is referred to as a *mixture* of the two distributions. The inequality then says that the entropy of the mixture of the two distributions is at least as great as corresponding mixture of the two entropies.

Entropy of Shares

As entropy provides us with a quantification of the degree to which a unit of probability is unevenly divided among n outcomes, it is natural to use the same idea to quantify how unevenly the total income pie is divided in a population. Assume that the population individuals have incomes $y_1, \ldots, y_n$, so that the share of income for person i is $s_i = y_i / n\bar{y}$, with these shares summing to unity $\sum_{i=1}^{n} s_i = 1$. We treat these shares like probabilities and define as a measure of income inequality the quantity $H = -\sum_{i=1}^{n} s_i \log(s_i)$. (Observe that we use the natural logarithm here.)

Entropy-Based Inequality Measures

When we introduced the Gini coefficient, we measured the area between the Lorenz curve and the equality line (which corresponds to the case of complete equality). In a similar manner, we can compute the difference between the entropy obtained in case of complete equality, where each person receives an equal income share, and the entropy defined for the actual income shares. The resulting measure is referred to as the *Theil inequality index:*

$$T = H(1/n, \ldots, 1/n) - H(s_1, \ldots, s_n) = -\sum_{i=1}^{n} \frac{1}{n} \log\left(\frac{1}{n}\right) + \sum_{i=1}^{n} s_i \log(s_i). \quad (3.8a)$$

$$T = \sum_{i=1}^{n} s_i \left[\log(s_i) - \log\left(\frac{1}{n}\right) \right]. \quad (3.8b)$$

$$T = \frac{1}{n} \sum_{i=1}^{n} \frac{y_i}{\bar{y}} \left[\log\left(\frac{y_i}{\bar{y}}\right) \right]. \quad (3.8c)$$

These three expressions for the index are equivalent.[7] Equation 3.8c shows the ratio of income to the mean income $y_i / \bar{y}$. is a fundamental

---

[7]The middle steps before Equation 3.7a and b are as follows:

$$T = -\sum_{i=1}^{n} \frac{1}{n} \log\left(\frac{1}{n}\right) + \sum_{i=1}^{n} s_i \log(s_i) = -\log\left(\frac{1}{n}\right) + \sum_{i=1}^{n} s_i \log(s_i)$$

$$= -\log\left(\frac{1}{n}\right) \sum_{i=1}^{n} s_i + \sum_{i=1}^{n} s_i \log(s_i) = \sum_{i=1}^{n} s_i \left[\log(s_i) - \log\left(\frac{1}{n}\right) \right]$$

element underlying the definition. As in the case of the logarithmic variance or the Atkinson index, the income ratio guarantees that the Theil's inequality index is scale invariant.

Since Theil's inequality index is the complete equality entropy minus the measured entropy, its value lies in the interval $[0, \log(n)]$, with 0 indicating complete equality and $\log(n)$ the extreme inequality (one person has the total income). Thus, while entropy is maximized for the case when all probabilities are equal, this corresponds to the minimum value of Theil's inequality index, where all the shares are equal.

The concavity property of entropy leads immediately to a property of Theil's inequality index that is quite intuitively appealing. Consider two policies by which a population shares its total income. Under the first policy, let the sharing proportions be denoted by $(p_1, \ldots, p_n)$, and under the second policy, let these be denoted by $(q_1, \ldots, q_n)$. Thus, under the first policy, individual i receives a proportion p_i of the total income, and under the second policy, this proportion is q_i. Now we can define a new sharing policy by using the average proportions under these two basic policies, so that individual i receives $\frac{1}{2}(p_i + q_i)$. The concavity property of entropy then guarantees that Theil's inequality index under the combined policy is no greater than the average of the Theil's indices for the two policies:

$$T_{\text{combined policy}} \leq \frac{1}{2}(T_{\text{Policy 1}} + T_{\text{Policy 2}}).$$

More generally, we can form a weighted average of the two policies. Pick any constant λ between 0 and 1, and assign for every individual a share equal to the weighted average of the shares under Policies 1 and 2, that is, individual i receives a share of $\lambda p_i + (1 - \lambda)q_i$. The concavity property of entropy guarantees that Theil's measure of inequality is never greater than the corresponding weighted average of the Theil's inequality measures under the two policies, that is,

$$T_{\text{combined policy}} \leq \lambda T_{\text{Policy 1}} + (1 - \lambda)T_{\text{Policy 2}}.$$

Row 13 of Table 3.1 shows the Theil inequality index for the symmetric distribution of income and its four shifted distributions. The index takes the value of .022 for the symmetrically distributed income and is the same for the scale-shifted distribution. The index decreases after a positive location shift and a left-skewed shift but increases after a right-skewed shift. Similarly, Row 13 of Table 3.2 shows the increase in the Theil inequality index from 0.244 in 1991 to 0.310 in 2001.

The logarithmic transformation of income shares in entropy and the Theil index is but one example in a family of transformations. Cowell (2000,

p. 52) describes a family of modified information-theoretic measures, where a more general definition of entropy is used:

$$GE_\theta = \frac{1}{\theta^2 - \theta} \left[\frac{1}{n} \sum_{i=1}^{n} \left(\frac{y_i}{\bar{y}} \right)^\theta - 1 \right], \tag{3.9}$$

where θ is a sensitivity parameter whose value can be any real number, positive, zero, or negative. The more positive the θ is, the more sensitive the index is to income differences at the top of the distribution, referred to as "top-sensitive" generalized entropy indexes. Similarly, the more negative the θ is, the more sensitive the index is to differences at the bottom of the distribution, referred to as "bottom-sensitive" generalized entropy indexes. As with the Theil index, the generalized entropy is scale invariant.

When $\theta = 1$, $\theta = 0$, or $\theta = 2$, special forms are derived from Equation 3.9 (see Chapter 3, Appendix B, posted on the authors' Web site). When $\theta = 1$, we obtain the Theil index:

$$G^1E_1 = \frac{1}{n} \sum_{i=1}^{n} \left(\frac{y_i}{\bar{y}} \right) \log \left(\frac{y_i}{\bar{y}} \right) = T.$$

When $\theta = 0$, we have

$$GE_0 = \frac{-1}{n} \sum_{i=1}^{n} \log \left(\frac{y_i}{\bar{y}} \right),$$

which is known as the mean log deviation. When $\theta = 2$, we get $GE_2 = c^2/2$, which is half of the squared coefficient of variation. Other special values of θ are ordinally related to familiar inequality measures. When $\theta = -1$, the generalized entropy is related to the mean of the inverse individual attributes. When $0 < \theta < 1$, the generalized entropy has an ordinal relationship with Atkinson indexes. For every member of the Atkinson family (defined by the inequality aversion parameter), there is an ordinally equivalent member in the generalized entropy family. However, the opposite is not true since θ can take any value outside the $(0,1)$ range.

Rows 14 to 17 in Table 3.1 list four special cases of the generalized entropy. In Row 14, Theil's index is the same as GE_1 at $\theta = 1$. As θ decreases from 1 to 0 and −1 in Rows 14 to 16, we see the increasing values of GE_θ for the symmetric distribution of income and its four shifted distributions. In Row 17, we see that GE_2 is half of the coefficient of variation squared ($c^2/2$). The generalized entropy remains the same after a scale shift. The U.S. income inequalities measured by generalized entropy are shown in Rows 14 to 17 in Table 3.2. We are reminded that the temporal trend of generalized entropy must be examined using the same sensitivity parameter θ. For example, a bottom-sensitive GE_{-1} not only shows a much greater degree of inequality in 1991 and 2001 but also exhibits a greater rate of growth of inequality between the two years than $GE_1 = T$, which focuses on the middle portion of the distribution.

Generalized entropy measures have many useful properties. But above all, generalized entropy is sufficiently flexible to characterize inequality in a manner that may be tailored to a variety of specific substantive needs, while upholding all the basic principles for inequality measures.

Inequality Measures for Variables With Nonpositive Values

So far we have treated income or other resources as containing no negative or zero values. Much empirical research pays attention to the distribution of positive values of income, because the proportion of population with negative income (e.g., due to capital loss) or no income is typically very small. A practice in empirical work is to delete cases with negative or zero values. The situation is quite different for wealth, which is measured by net worth (total assets minus total debts). The proportion of households without positive total net worth is substantial (17% in 2001 from our SIPP data). For instance, negative net worth due to student loans stems from life cycle differences. People smooth consumption by entailing credit card debts. Housing market bubbles and the following crises can drastically drop a house's value relative to its mortgage, resulting in negative home equity. Financial market crises can drastically reduce the value of people's investments in stocks and bonds. Thus, households with negative or zero total worth are too important to delete.

Not all inequality measures reviewed here can handle negative or zero values of the outcome variable; those inequality measures using the logarithm function cannot deal with nonpositive values, neither can some of the Atkinson indices and generalized entropy family except for GE_2. Variance, coefficient of variation, Gini coefficient, and quantile-based measures can be used to examine wealth inequality in these cases.

Table 3.3 shows inequality measures that can handle negative and zero net worth values using SIPP 1991 and 2001 wealth data. The proportion of households with negative net worth is 8.4% and that with zero net worth is 4.4%, totaling 12.8% of households having no positive net worth in 1991. The corresponding numbers for 2001 are 12.9%, 4.3%, and 17.1%, respectively. The range and standard deviation increase tremendously over the 10 years, reflecting the much greater differentiation in net worth in 2001 than in 1991. The coefficient of variation jumps from 1.73 to 8.84, mainly reflecting the growth in variance (although the median net worth gains \$6,303 adjusting the c in 2001 by a small factor). The quantile range $p95$ to $p5$ also increases by almost half. Note that $p5$ is a negative value since more than 5% of households have negative net worth in both years. We do not use the quantile-based skewness because of the approximately 4% households with zero values, which makes the net worth distribution multimodal. The total net worth for the bottom 20% is a negative value for both years (the sum of negative net worth is larger than the sum of positive net worth), resulting in a negative share, -0.010 in 1991 and -0.018 in 2001. The share for the top 20% households grew from 0.699 to 0.766. The Gini coefficient also grew from 0.700 to 0.769.

	Inequality Measures	1991	2001
	Related to the probability distribution		
1	R (range) in \$1,000	6,850	221,977
2	$\sqrt{V}$ (standard deviation) in \$1,000	200	1,458
3	c (coefficient of variation)	1.730	8.840
	Based on quantile functions and Lorenz curves		
6	$p95$ to $p5$ (quantile range) in \$1,000	463	664
8	Share of bottom fifth	−0.010	−0.018
9	Share of top fifth	0.699	0.766
10	G (Gini coefficient)	0.700	0.769
	Percentage negative values	8.4	12.9
	Percentage zero value	4.4	4.2
	Median (in \$)	45,843	52,146

Table 3.3 Inequality Measures for Household Net Worth: SIPP 1991 and 2001

Note: SIPP, Survey of Income and Program Participation.

Summary

This chapter introduces a set of selected summary inequality measures. Appendix Table 3.A1 lists the name and the formula for each. We discuss the basic rationale behind each measure and link them through location, scale, and shape shifts, illustrated with both hypothetical and real-world examples. Choices of inequality measures for specific research will depend on the principles that allow us to compare inequality measures in various ways. We turn to this topic in the next chapter.

Appendix

Name	Formula
Related to probability distribution	
Range	$R = y_{\max} - y_{\min}$
Variance	$V = \dfrac{1}{n} \sum_{i=1}^{n} (y_i - \bar{y})^2$
Coefficient of variation	$c = \dfrac{\sqrt{V}}{\bar{y}}$
Logarithmic variance	$v = \dfrac{1}{n} \sum_{i=1}^{n} \left(\log\left(\dfrac{y_i}{\bar{y}}\right) \right)^2 = \dfrac{1}{n} \sum_{i=1}^{n} (\log y_i - \log \bar{y})^2$
Variance of logarithms	$v_1 = \dfrac{1}{n} \sum_{i=1}^{n} \left(\log\left(\dfrac{y_i}{y^*}\right) \right)^2 = \dfrac{1}{n} \sum_{i=1}^{n} \left(\log(y_i) - \overline{\log(y)} \right)^2$
Based on quantile function and Lorenz curve	
Quantile ratio	$Q^p / Q^{p'}$ for $p \neq p'$
Share measures	
Lower quantile interval	$L(p)$
Middle quantile interval	$L(p_U) - L(p_L)$
Upper quantile interval	$1 - L(1 - p)$
Gini coefficient	$G = \dfrac{\displaystyle\sum_{1 \leq j \leq i \leq n}^{n} |y_i - y_j|}{n(n-1)\bar{y}}$

Name	Formula
Based on social welfare function	
Atkinson index	$A_\varepsilon = 1 - \left[\dfrac{1}{n} \sum\limits_{i=1}^{n} \left(\dfrac{y_i}{\bar{y}} \right)^{1-\varepsilon} \right]^{\frac{1}{1-\varepsilon}}$
Based on information theory	
Theil index	$T = \dfrac{1}{n} \sum\limits_{i=1}^{n} \dfrac{y_i}{\bar{y}} \left[\log \left(\dfrac{y_i}{\bar{y}} \right) \right]$
Generalized entropy	$GE_\theta = \dfrac{1}{\theta^2 - \theta} \left[\dfrac{1}{n} \sum\limits_{i=1}^{n} \left(\dfrac{y_i}{\bar{y}} \right)^{\theta} - 1 \right]$

Table 3.A1 Selected Summary Inequality Measures

CHAPTER 4. CHOICES OF INEQUALITY MEASURES

Some summary inequality measures discussed in Chapter 3 are families of indexes, and each family involves a parameter that can take on many values. Given this large number of summary inequality measures, how do we choose one or several to meet the needs of a specific study? Knowing whether an inequality measure satisfies certain principles that are desirable for a specific study is a good first step. We now turn to a discussion of these principles, including the weak principle of transfers, the strong principle of transfers, scale invariance, the principle of population, and decomposability. We will define these principles, explain why they are important for selecting inequality measures, and check whether each inequality measure discussed in Chapter 3 satisfies these principles. Empirical examples for these principles are also provided. After introducing the five principles, we discuss theoretical and practical considerations for choosing inequality measures for examining one population. Finally, we bring up the Lorenz dominance as an overarching guideline for comparing populations.

Weak Principle of Transfers

The principle of transfers first introduced by Dalton (1920) is now referred to as the *weak* principle of transfers, and concerns the change in social welfare after a transfer between two members of society, as discussed in Chapter 3. Consider the following scenario. A transfer is made from a poorer person to a richer person while keeping both the total income as well as the post-transfer ranking of the two persons relative to one another unchanged; that is, less than a half of the difference of their income is transferred. Any transfer from a poorer person to a richer person, other things remaining the same, should always increase an inequality measure (Sen, 1973). This principle is called the Pigou-Dalton transfer principle. Sen wrote,

> In fact as early as 1920, Hugh Dalton had argued that any measure of inequality must have this minimal property and since in this Dalton was following a lead of Pigou, whom he quoted in this context, we shall call this the Pigou-Dalton condition. (p. 27)

This condition is now termed the weak principle of transfer, which states that a transfer from a richer person to a poorer person, other things being equal, leads to a reduction of inequality.

Many inequality measures reviewed in Chapter 3 obey the weak principle of transfer. As discussed in detail in Chapter 3, the Atkinson family of indexes and the general entropy family of measures satisfy this principle.

The Gini coefficient G is also ordinally equivalent to Atkinson indexes (Sen, 1976), so it also satisfies this principle.

However, the logarithmic variance v and the variance of the logarithms v_1 do not always obey the weak principle of transfers. It is possible to state some results that explain how transfers affect the logarithmic variance v. These rely on a certain condition regarding the upper tail of the income distribution, which states that all of the income levels in the population are at most $\bar{y}e$, where $\bar{y}$ denotes the population mean, and $e = 2.71828\ldots$. This condition states that the maximum income level is not too extreme relative to the mean income. For right-skewed distributions of income or other resources, it is unusual for the maximum to be less than three times the mean which would cause the condition to fail. In any case, if the income distribution satisfies this condition, then for any pair of individuals i and j with incomes satisfying $y_i < y_j$, inequality as measured by v declines when we transfer an income amount $\delta < \frac{1}{2}(y_j - y_i)$ from person j to person i. On the other hand, when the condition fails, for any pair of individuals i and j whose incomes satisfy $\bar{y}e < y_i < y_j$, the transfer of an income amount $\delta < \frac{1}{2}(y_j - y_i)$ from person j to person i causes inequality, as measured by v, to increase. The reason why the variance of logs v_1 does not satisfy the weak principle of transfers is more intuitive (Foster & Ok, 1999). Because transfers are defined so as not to change the total income, the mean income $\bar{y}$ used in most inequality measures (except v_1) does not change either. However, the mean of log income changes after a transfer. If the change in mean of log income outweighs the changes in individual income, v_1 may increase after a rich-to-poor transfer. This condition is also unlikely to happen if transfers are not within the very top tail.

For example, using the Survey of Income and Program Participation (SIPP) 2001 data, we artificially create a rich-to-poor transfer under the condition of $\bar{y}e < y_i < y_j$ for logarithmic variance v to increase after a transfer from y_j to y_i. We rank the households by income to identify 1,096 (4%) households having income greater than $\bar{y}e = \$136,822$. Then the highest-ranked household gives the lowest-ranked household within the top 4% \$290,000 (which is smaller than one half of their income difference). After the transfer, the giver is still richer than the receiver. The pretransfer $v = 0.96850$ and the posttransfer $v = 0.96854$, indicating an increase despite the rich-to-poor transfer. Similarly, the variance of the logs also increases. Meanwhile, the variance, the coefficient of variation, the Gini coeffecient Atkinson's indices, and the generalized entropy measures all decline.

Quantile-based inequality measures may also fail the weak principle of transfers. A transfer between two individuals with incomes between the two relevant quantiles defining the measure should not change the measure. Using the above example of a rich-to-poor transfer within the top 4%, we find that the $p95$

to $p5$ range, the quantile-based skewness for the middle 90% of households, the share of bottom fifth, and the share of top fifth all remain the same since the transfer was made within the top 4%. Despite the failure of the weak principle of transfers, quantile-based measures are commonly used in both government statistics and academic research. The main advantage of using quantile-based measures is that quantiles are not affected by outliers or top coding routinely practiced in public-used survey data. In the case of $p95$ to $p5$ range, so long as the top coding is above $p95$, the range is not affected by top coding. In contrast, top coding does affect summary inequality measures based on all data points, including the top-coded ones.

Strong Principle of Transfers

While the weak principle of transfers states that the posttransfer income distribution is less unequal than the pretransfer distribution, it does not tell us the degree to which the inequality changes when the transfer is made. It seems reasonable to require that a fixed amount transferred between two individuals separated by the same "distance" should yield the same reduction in inequality. In other words, for a transfer at a fixed distance, the resulting change in inequality depends only on the income shares of the donor and recipient. Therefore, one can compare different indexes in terms of the "distance between income shares" that each index incorporates. This leads to the *strong principle of transfers*. To satisfy the strong principle of transfers, inequality measures are required to satisfy the weak principle of transfers. The strong principle of transfers states that a transfer reduces inequality and that the amount of inequality reduction is the same if the same transfer is made between two persons of the same *distance,* regardless of the position of the giver and the receiver in the income distribution. The term *distance* must be interpreted with care, since, for a given inequality measure to satisfy the strong principle of transfers, a way to measure distance must be specified.

All the *distances* we consider are obtained by using the absolute difference, or the absolute difference after making a transformation, or by ranking. The most basic distance to consider is the simple absolute difference measure, $s_2 - s_1$, when the richer person's income is s_2 and the poorer person's income is s_1. Using this measure of distance, the variance V satisfies the strong principle of transfers. On the other hand, the coefficient of variation c does not satisfy the principle with this measure of distance because, as can be verified, the change in c resulting from a transfer between individuals whose income differs by a fixed amount depends on the value of V.

Other distance measures relative to which an inequality measure satisfies the strong principle are defined using the distance above after applying an income transformation. An example is the absolute difference between two log-transformed income shares. The Theil index T uses the log transformation of income, thus the distance between two persons' incomes is the log distance: $\log(s_2) - \log(s_1)$. Note also that the special case of the generalized entropy GE_1 is equivalent to T; consequently the log distance applies to GE_1. For generalized entropy with a specified value of θ a different transformation is used that involves a power function of the income shares:

$$\frac{s_1^{\theta-1}}{\theta-1} - \frac{s_2^{\theta-1}}{\theta-1}.$$

This power distance reduces to the absolute distance $s_2 - s_1$ when $\theta = 2$, and to the log distance when $\theta = 1$. For the Atkinson family of indices, a transfer of a small amount δ from individual j to i leads to the change of approximately $\delta\,(U'(y_2) - U'(y_1))$ in the inequality measure, so these measures can be said to satisfy an *infinitesimal* version of the strong principle of transfers based on the distance defined in terms of the social utility function as $U'(y_2) - U'(y_1)$. There is not a natural distance measure associated with the Gini coefficient for which a property resembling the strong principle holds.

The strong this principle guarantees the same reduction in inequality for a transfer between two individuals both located within the lower tail, both near the median, or both located in the upper tail, so long as the distance (specific for that index) of separation between them is the same. This property is needed if research is concerned with both the rank and the magnitude of the change in inequality ("cardinal" properties), but it might be too restrictive if a researcher's main concern is ordinal when comparing distributions.

Among the inequality measures reviewed in Chapter 3, generalized entropy measures (including the Theil index and the squared coefficient of variation) satisfy the strong principle of transfers. No other reviewed inequality measures satisfy this principle.

Scale Invariance

The scale-invariance issue was mentioned during our introduction to the inequality measures in Chapter 3. An inequality measure is said to be scale invariant if it remains unchanged after a scale shift, a fixed percentage increase (or decrease) in income for everyone in the population. All inequality measures that are normalized using the mean income, total income, or any arbitrary income (e.g., the geometric mean income and the median income) possess this property (see Appendix Table 4.1). The c, V, G, T, A_ε, and GE_θ are normalized by the mean income $\bar{y}$; the v_1 is normalized by the mean log income $\overline{\log(y)}$, the quantile-based skewness measure is normalized by the median income; and the income shares are normalized by the total income. In contrast, the range R, variance V, and quantile ranges are not scale invariant.

Principle of Population

Investigation of time trends in income inequality for a population is complicated by the fact that the population may be growing from one period to the next. We seek ways of measuring income inequality that is independent of such growth. For some research, the *size* of the population should not affect the quantification of the inequality trend of a society or the inequality patterns across societies. The principle of population says that when we measure income inequality in a population, this measurement depends only on the *distribution* of income in the population. Arguably, one could measure social welfare by, for example, counting the number of individuals in the population who are considered in poverty, but historically, this type of analysis has not been the focus of inequality studies. The population principle is related to the idea of per capita income seen in government statistics and academic research.

One can do a simple exercise to illustrate the principle of population. The total sample of SIPP 2001 is $n = 27,294$. We double the sample size of the SIPP data by creating a mirror household for each household in the sample so that the sample size is now $2n = 54,588$. Clearly, the per capita income remains unchanged. We then recalculate the inequality measures reviewed in Chapter 3 and observe that they are the same in both the n-size case and the $2n$-size case. This illustrates that the selected inequality measures reviewed satisfy the principle of population.

Decomposability

A society is typically stratified into various groups by race, gender, education levels, age, and other factors. We then view some differences between individual members of society as being explained by the fact that they fall into different strata, while recognizing the possibility for differences among individuals within the same strata. As such, we anticipate the possibility of *decomposing* a given inequality measure, so that the total income inequality is partitioned into the between-group inequality (e.g., between blacks and whites) and within-group inequality (e.g., inequality among whites and inequality among blacks). Another type of decomposition arises quite naturally in applications. For instance, income can come from different sources, for example, earned income and unearned income, in which case it is of interest to know how the total income inequality is partitioned between and within income sources.

An inequality measure is said to be additively decomposable if it can be expressed as the between-group inequality plus the weighted sum of the inequality within each group. Here, we allow for the possibility that the weights depend on the within group means and the overall mean. We proceed to describe which of the reviewed inequality measures are additively decomposable and in each case we provide explicit decompositions. This requires some care as it entails identifying both the weights as well and the measure of between group inequality.

Variance provides a familiar and illustrative notion of additive decomposition. We know that the total variance is the sum of the between-variance and the weighted sum of the within-variances. We apply this law to the empirical data for a white group of size m and a black group of size n. The total income of the sample has a mean $\bar{y}$ and an unbiased variance V^T. The white income has a mean $\bar{y}_{\text{wht}}$ and a unbiased variance $V_{\text{wht,}}$ and the black income has a mean $\bar{y}_{\text{blk}}$ and an unbiased variance V_{blk}.

The between variance, V^B can be obtained by changing each of the m whites' incomes to $\bar{y}_{\text{wht}}$ and each of the n blacks' incomes to $\bar{y}_{\text{blk}}$ and then taking the variance of the resulting data. The within component, V^W is the weighted sum of the within variances. Because the unbiased variance adjusts for the sample size ($m + n - 1$ for the total, $m - 1$ for whites and $n - 1$ for blacks), we need to account for this in the weights used for each group's variance. In particular, the weight for whites becomes the adjusted white proportion $(m - 1)/(m + n - 1)$, and the weight for blacks becomes the adjusted black proportion $(n - 1)/(m + n - 1)$. Note that the two weights do not add up to unity. With this setup, we can express the additive decomposition of variance based on empirical data as:

$$V^T = V^B + V^W$$

$$= V^B + \frac{m - 1}{m + n - 1} V_{\text{wht}} + \frac{n - 1}{m + n - 1} V_{\text{blk}}. \quad (4.1)$$

As the coefficient of variation c is the standard deviation normalized by the mean, its squared term c^2 is also additively decomposable. c^2 is the variance of total income normalized by the square of the grand mean. The between coefficient of variation squared c^{2B} is obtained in a similar manner as for the between variance by assigning every white member with the white mean income and every black member with the black mean income. The normalization of this between term is also by the square of the grand mean. However, since the group squared coefficients of variation c_{wht}^2 and c_{blk}^2 are normalized by the squares of the respective group means, and not the square of the overall mean, a compound weight that combines the adjusted group proportion and the square of the group-to-grand mean ratio must be used. Specifically, the compound weight is $[(m - 1)/(m + n - 1)](\bar{y}_{\text{wht}}/\bar{y})^2$

for whites and $(n-1)/(m+n-1)](\bar{y}_{\text{blk}}/\bar{y})^2$ for blacks. Thus, the additive decomposition of c^2 can be expressed as

$$
\begin{aligned}
c^{2T} &= c^{2B} + c^{2W} \\
&= c^{2B} + \left(\frac{m-1}{m+n-1}\right)\left(\frac{\bar{y}_{\text{wht}}}{\bar{y}}\right)^2 c_{\text{wht}}^2 + \left(\frac{n-1}{m+n-1}\right)\left(\frac{\bar{y}_{\text{blk}}}{\bar{y}}\right)^2 c_{\text{blk}}^2. \quad (4.2)
\end{aligned}
$$

The Theil inequality index T is additively decomposable. The total Theil index T^T is the between component plus the within component. The between Theil T^B is obtained in a similar manner to the between variance and the square of the between coefficient of variation, by assigning every white member the mean white income and every black member the mean black income. However, the weights for the within component T^W are different than those in V or c^2. The weight is the group income share of the total income: $[m\bar{y}_{\text{wht}}/(m+n)\bar{y}] = [m/(m+n)](\bar{y}_{\text{wht}}/\bar{y})$ for whites and $[n/(m+n)](\bar{y}_{\text{blk}}/\bar{y})$ for blacks. The additive decomposition for Theil is then

$$
\begin{aligned}
T^T &= T^B + T^W \\
&= T^B + \frac{m}{m+n}\frac{\bar{y}_{\text{wht}}}{\bar{y}}T_{\text{wht}} + \frac{n}{m+n}\frac{\bar{y}_{\text{blk}}}{\bar{y}}T_{\text{blk}}. \quad (4.3)
\end{aligned}
$$

The square of the coefficient of variation and the Theil inequality index are special cases of the generalized entropy. In this chapter's appendix (on the authors' Web site for this book), we show that the generalized entropy can be additively decomposed into a between component and a within component. Using the same example of income data with black-white grouping, we have the following general expression:

$$
\begin{aligned}
GE_\theta^T &= GE_\theta^B + GE_\theta^W \\
&= GE_\theta^T + \frac{m}{m+n}\left(\frac{\bar{y}_{\text{wht}}}{\bar{y}}\right)^\theta GE_\theta^{\text{wht}} + \frac{n}{m+n}\left(\frac{\bar{y}_{\text{blk}}}{\bar{y}}\right)^\theta GE_\theta^{\text{blk}}. \quad (4.4)
\end{aligned}
$$

Note that in Equation 4.4, the two weights do not generally sum to one. Expression 4.4 Equation generalizes 4.2 and 4.3 and applies to every measure in the generalized entropy family.

Using Equations 4.1 to 4.4 and the SIPP 2001 income data for blacks and whites, we decompose V, c^2, and T (see Table 4.1). The total sample size is 23,585, with the black proportion of 0.1443. The mean income is $50,911 for the total, $53,655 for whites, and $35,198 for blacks. For these measures, the total inequality is the sum of the between inequality and the within component (weighted sum of the within inequality). It is straightforward to obtain the three inequality measures for the total sample, the white sample, and the black sample. To create the between inequality measures, we create a new income variable by assigning to each white person the mean white income and to each black person the mean black income. The weight for each racial group differs across the three inequality measures. Take the weight for whites as an example. For V, the weight for whites is the adjusted white group proportion $(m - 1)/(m + n - 1) = (23585(1 - 0.1443) - 1)/(23585 - 1) = 0.8557$. Because the sample size is large, this adjusted group proportion is very close to the unadjusted group proportion. The white and black weights seem to sum to 1, but this is due to the large sample sizes. The adjustment is only important for small sample sizes. For c^2, the weight for whites is the weight for V multiplied by $(\bar{y}_{\text{wht}}/\bar{y})^2$, resulting in 0.9474. Note that the weights for the two racial groups do not sum to 1. For T, the weight for whites is $[m/(m + n)](\bar{y}_{\text{wht}}/\bar{y}) = 0.9004$. The weights for whites and blacks sum to 1 in this case. This example illustrates the various weights associated with different inequality measures. The additive decomposition results in Table 4.2 indicate that the major source of total inequality is the within component (97%–98%) and the between white-black inequality accounts for only a small fraction of the total inequality (2%–3%).

Two Stata modules for decomposing inequality measures are available: "ineqdeco" requires that the outcome variable be positive, and "ineqdec0" allows for variables taking any values (Jenkins, 1999). For illustration, non-positive values have been removed from the SIPP 2001 income data. We use "ineqdeco" in Stata to obtain the subgroup decomposition for the generalized entropy family and the Atkinson family in 1991 and 2001. The results are shown in Table 4.2. While the generalized entropy family is additively decomposable, the Atkinson family is not. However, we can decompose the Atkinson index as a sum of a between component, a within component, and a *residual* which is minus the product of the between and within components. We add a residual column in Table 4.2 for each value of the Atkinson index. The table does not present decomposition of the Gini coefficient G, the logarithmic variance v, and the variance of the logarithms v_1, because they are not additively decomposable, and the residual component cannot be obtained with the between and within terms as in the case of the Atkinson index.

The method for decomposing inequality by population subgroups can be directly applied to population subregions. For example, if we wish to

Inequality Measure	Total	Between	White	Black	Weight for White	Weight for Black	Weighted Sum of Within	Total – (Between + Weighted Within)
V	2,077 (100%)	42 (2%)	2,212	989	0.8557	0.1443	2035 (98%)	0
c^2	0.7989 (100%)	0.0162 (2%)	0.7682	0.7983	0.9474	0.0688	0.7827 (98%)	0.0000
T	0.3073 (100%)	0.0089 (3%)	0.2955	0.3239	0.9004	0.0996	0.2983 (97%)	0.0000

Table 4.1 Illustrating Additive Decomposition of Three Inequality Measures for Income with Black-White Grouping: SIPP 2001

Note: The sample includes only blacks and whites, totaling 23,585 households. The proportion is .0.1443 for blacks. The mean income is $50,911 for the total, $53,655 for whites, and $35,198 for blacks. Variance is in million dollars-squared. See the text for ways to obtain the weights for each group. SIPP, Survey of Income and Program Participation.

Term	1991				2001			
	Total	Between	Within	Residual	Total	Between	Within	Residual
GE_{-1}	1.442	0.012	1.430	0	3.022	0.011	3.011	0
GE_0	0.284	0.010	0.273	0	0.345	0.010	0.335	0
GE_1	0.240	0.009	0.231	0	0.307	0.009	0.298	0
GE_2	0.267	0.008	0.259	0	0.399	0.008	0.391	0
$A_{1/2}$	0.121	0.006	0.116	-0.001	0.148	0.005	0.144	-0.001
A_1	0.247	0.014	0.237	-0.004	0.292	0.012	0.283	-0.003
A_2	0.742	0.037	0.733	-0.028	0.858	0.116	0.839	-0.097

Table 4.2 Decomposition of Inequality Measures for Income with Black-White Grouping: SIPP 1991 and 2001

Note: SIPP, Survey of Income and Program Participation.

compare income inequality in the South and the non-South as measured by the generalized entropy or the Atkinson family of indexes, we use the same methods discussed above.

Much empirical work on inequality decomposition focuses on population subgroups. Income or wealth is comprised of various components. For example, income sources include earnings, investment income, welfare payments, private transfers, and capital gains/losses. Wealth components include the home, stocks and mutual funds, savings and checking accounts, and retirement funds. It is useful to understand how the between-component variation and the within-component variation contribute to the total income or the total net worth. Unlike the problem of decomposition by subgroups, there are relatively few inequality measures that allow for a convenient breakdown by components of income or wealth. The squared coefficient of variation c^2 and measures that are ordinally equivalent to it (such as variance V) allow for decomposition by components (Cowell, 2000). To show this, we use an example of net worth y_i, which is total assets minus total debts, a measure of total wealth. For simplicity, we define two components—the net worth of the home y_{Ai} and the net worth of all else y_{Bi}, such that $y_i = y_{Ai} + y_{Bi}$. Now let c, c_A, and c_B be the value of the coefficient of variation for total, home, and other net worth. Let λ be the proportion for the A component and ρ be the correlation coefficient between component A and component B. The decomposition of c is

$$c^2 = \lambda^2 c_A^2 + (1 - \lambda)^2 c_B^2 + 2\lambda(1 - \lambda)c_A c_B \rho. \qquad (4.5)$$

Since $GE_{(2)} = c^2/2$, we can express Equation 4.5 in terms of $GE_{(2)}$:

$$GE_{(2)} = \lambda^2 GE_{A(2)} + (1 - \lambda)^2 GE_{A(2)} + 2\lambda(1 - \lambda)\rho\sqrt{GE_{A(2)}GE_{B(2)}}. \qquad (4.5')$$

Equations 4.5 and 4.5' can be applied to any value range of the resource variable, so it is appropriate for net worth, which has a substantial proportion of negative and zero values. Using the SIPP 1991 and 2001 wealth data, the results are shown in Table 4.3. Because of the negative and zero values of net worth, the coefficient of variation is not directly comparable to the one based on only positive values of the response variable. The first three rows suggest that the growth in the coefficient of variation from 1.729 to 8.841 largely reflects the growth in inequality of nonhouse net worth: from 2.518 to 14.383. Component decompositions in Table 4.3, that is, the proportions of the total that each term represents, can reveal interesting trends—the total home equity was 45.1% in 1991 and dropped to 39.0% in 2001—and the correlation between the two components, which declined from .352 to .073. Based on these basic statistics, we found that the weighted contribution of home equity dropped from 14.6% to 0.5%, whereas the weighted contribution of the nonhome net worth rose from 63.9% to 98.4%. The third term in (4.5) arises from the correlation between components and reduced to only 1% from 21.5%. The decomposition, when expressed in terms of percentages, provides a direct comparison between the two distributions and identify the major source of rising inequality.[1]

While the Gini coefficient does not satisfy the additive decomposability principle, some researchers view the nonadditivity as an advantage rather than a limitation. Two distinctive decomposition frameworks are *additive* and *interactive*. Under the additive decomposition framework, the between-group component captures the mean difference between two groups and the within-group component captures the remaining variation. Under the inter-active decomposition framework, a group's characteristics can be conceived as the group's central location and its distributional shape. Different central locations and shapes can result in different degrees of group overlapping. Consider a population consisting of two racial groups—whites and blacks. Not only is the black-white mean income gap wide but the distributional shapes also differ. In particular, in the region where the black distribution and the white distribution overlap, some blacks have higher income than whites. Both the mean income difference and the group overlapping can be conceived as between-group differences. If one is interested in not only how the mean income differs but also how the two groups overlap (some blacks have higher income than some whites), the Gini decomposition can be used to extract some relevant information.

Three methods have been proposed to decompose Gini: (1) a graphic method (Lambert & Aroson, 1993), (2) a covariance method (Lerman & Yitzhaki, 1984; Sastry & Kelkar, 1994), and (3) a pairwise individual income comparison method (Dagum, 1997; Mussard, Terraza, & Seyte, 2003). Regardless of the methods, Gini decompositions emphasize the overlap of groups and the substantive meaning behind it, and offer additional information that is absent in the additive decomposition of other inequality measures.

Using the same white and black sample from the SIPP 2001 income data, we calculate that the overall Gini coefficient is 0.4221, which is decomposed into three components: The between component (black-white mean income gap or the gross variation between the two groups) accounts for 10.6% of the total Gini; the within component (weighted sum of inequality within each group) accounts for 77.2%; and the overlapping component (the fact that

---

[1]Lerman and Yitzhaki (1984) decompose the Gini coefficient by components. The decomposition equation is in a multiplicative form. From decomposition they obtain the marginal effect of 1% increase in a component on the Gini. Lopez-Feldman (2006) implemented the Lerman and Yitzhaki method in the Stata program "descogini." Using this module, we found that 1% increase in home equity would decrease the Gini by 5.7% in 1991 and such an effect would be stronger in 2001 (7.4%).

Term	1991	2001
Coefficient of variation, total c	1.729	8.841
Coefficient of variation, home c_A	1.466	1.630
Coefficient of variation, other c_B	2.518	14.383
Proportion for c_A: λ	0.451	0.390
Component correlation: ρ	0.352	0.073
Total: c_2	2.991 (100%)	78.159 (100%)
Part 1: $\lambda^2 c_A^2$	0.437 (14.6%)	0.405 (0.5%)
Part 2: $(1 - \lambda)^2 c_B^2$	1.911 (63.9%)	76.941 (98.4%)
Part 3: $2\lambda(1 - \lambda)c_A c_B \rho$	0.643 (21.5%)	0.814 (1.0%)

Table 4.3 Decomposition of Coefficient of Variation for Net Worth With Two Components: SIPP 1991 and 2001

Note: SIPP, Survey of Income and Program Participation.

some blacks have income higher than some whites, or the transvariation of the two groups) accounts for 12.2%. These results are very different from those using additive decomposition of, say Theil's index and the squared coefficient of variation, which have an overwhelming within-inequality share in the overall inequality (97%–98%). The between-group inequality accounts for a small percentage (2%–3%) of the overall inequality.

There are exceptional circumstances when groups, such as social classes, cluster along the income distribution, leading to a Gini decomposition with only between and within components (Liao, 2006). Social classes are defined as groups of individuals who are homogeneous within and heterogeneous between in income, education, and occupation, so that classes will be revealed in the form income clusters. The author creates ordered income clusters based on observed income, education attainment, and occupational prestige using model-based clustering (Fraley & Raftery, 1998). Because these clusters (classes) are ordered from low to high along the income distribution, no transvariation exists in cross-class pairwise individual comparisons. As a result, the Gini coefficient is decomposed into only two components—the between-class component and the within-class component—and there is no interactive component. Thus, a society where the income distribution has a sharp social class divide will have a large between-class component. Extending Gini decomposition to treating clusters along the income distribution provides a clear interpretation about how a society's income is stratified by social class using the relative contribution of the between-class component or a modified form of it. To further quantify the structure of inequality, Liao (2009) further develops structural inequality measures, including a disaggregate and an aggregative version of the structural Gini and a set of structural Theil measures.

Choose Inequality Measures for One Population

The five principles discussed above (see Appendix Table 4.A1) provide a set of basic criteria from which we choose one or several measures with desirable properties for a particular study. The choice is sometimes made for substantive reasons and sometimes for practical reasons.

Substantively, some research may concern itself with the sensitivity of the inequality measure used. The strong principle of transfers guarantees the same amount of reduction in inequality after a transfer of a fixed amount between two individuals who are a fixed distance apart, where the distance is specifically defined for different inequality measures. Thus, the strong principle emphasizes the size of transfer in terms of distances and the size of the change in the inequality measure. The notion of "cardinal" properties is used to describe such size-related changes. In comparison, the notion of "ordinal" properties is used to describe rank-related changes, what the weak principle of transfers emphasizes. When ordinal properties are of primary concern, we choose among various measures based on their sensitivity to different parts of the distribution. For example, the family of Atkinson indexes and the family of generalized entropy indexes are ordinally equivalent, when $0 < \theta < 1$ and $\theta = 1 - \varepsilon$. If we are primarily concerned with the ordinal property of the measure, we can choose either the Atkinson indexes or the generalized entropy with θ within the range of $(0,1)$ and focus on what value of ε or θ to use for the desired sensitivity. Extreme sensitivities would need the use of the generalized entropy with θ beyond the range of $(0,1)$. If we are concerned with the "cardinal" property (i.e., the size), then the generalized entropy is chosen.

Practically, the Gini index is the most widely used inequality measure. Two primary reasons for this popularity are its intuitive meaning obtained directly from Lorenz curves and its value range of $(0,1)$. When researchers are concerned with outliers and top or bottom coding of resources such as income and wealth, the Gini index is relatively robust as it is middle sensitive. In addition, when negative values are possible, as is often the case for income and wealth, the Gini index can handle these data, while the Atkinson family and most of the generalized entropy family cannot. Alternatively, the residual component after decomposing Gini is difficult to interpret. For research with a focus on decomposition, one may choose generalized entropy measures rather than the Gini.

Several inequality measures sharing common constituents can be used to deepen understanding of inequality phenomenon. Within the same population of size n, an individual income share can be expressed with the ratio of the individual income to the mean income $s_i = (1/n)(y_i/\bar{y})$. Using income ratio $y_i/\bar{y}$ as a common element in his unified framework for four summary inequality measures (squared coefficient of variation, variance of the logarithm, Theil index, and Gini coefficient), Firebaugh (1999) examines patterns of world income inequality. The unified framework expresses those inequality measures as a function of the income ratio measuring the average departure of the income ratio from the perfect equality case, when the ratio is 1.0 (see also Atkinson, 1970; Cowell, 2000; and Shorrocks 1980). This framework helps describe how the different functions lead to the different values of those inequality measures. In Firebaugh's study, three out of the four measures provide supporting evidence that the centuries-old trend of rising world income inequality leveled off from 1960 to 1989. The exception is variance of the logarithm v_1, which is more sensitive to changes at the lower end of income distribution because the log transformation compresses the right tail more than the lower tail, which actually showed a decline in world income inequality. This example shows that several inequality measures with a common element can be used to provide a deeper examination of the inequality pattern under consideration.

Finally, returning to location, scale, and shape shifts between two distributions, how do various summary inequality measures capture these shifts, and could they be disentangled? First, by definition, all scale-invariant summary inequality measures are designed to disentangle other shape shifts from scale shift. To capture scale shift, one should use inequality measures that are not scale invariant, such as variance and quantile ranges. Second, comparing the summary measures of two populations captures the combination of at least two distributional shifts—location shift and shape shift. To separate out the location shift from the shape shift (including scale shift for those measures that are not scale invariant), we can consider the two populations as two groups. We can then use a decomposable inequality measure to decompose the overall inequality measure into the between-group component and the within-group component. The between-group component captures the location shift, and the within-group component captures the shape shift. As shown in Table 4.1, the overall inequality of both black income and white income can be decomposed into location shift (the between component) and the shape shift (the within component) in V, c^2, and T. The result for V(variance) shows that the location shift accounts for 2% of the total distributional difference, whereas the scale and shape shifts combined account for 98%. The results for c^2 (squared coefficient of variation) and T (the Theil index) shows that the location shift accounts for 2.5% to 2.9% of the sum of location and shape shifts, regardless of any scale shift.

Lorenz Dominance and Population Comparison

Lorenz dominance is a strong condition that says conclusively that a distribution x is less unequal than a distribution y. This ability to be conclusive comes with a price: for a pair of distributions, it is possible that neither dominates the other, a condition we refer to as Lorenz intersection. Much research on income inequality is engaged in comparing income distributions among different countries, among states within the United States, across time periods, as well as among social groups based on race, gender, and age. In addition, research that compares effects of policy on income inequality concerns the reduction in inequality by a progressive transfer policy or the increase in inequality by a regressive transfer policy. This body of research shares a common concern: Which distribution is less unequal? Lorenz dominance provides a fundamental criterion for a credible answer to this question.

Based on the definition of the Lorenz curve in Chapter 2, we can say that Distribution **x** Lorenz dominates distribution **y** whenever $L_x(p) \geq L_y(p)$ holds for all $p \in [0, 1]$ (with $L_x(p) > L_y(p)$ for some p, that is, **x** and **y** are not identical). In other words, the Lorenz curve for **x** inside the region bounded by the equality line and the Lorenz curve for **y**. Figure 4.1 shows Lorenz dominance of **x** over **y**, each of which consists of five values (**x**={70, 80, 80, 80, 90} and **y**={30, 60, 80, 100, 130}). This example shows that for each of the five ps, the cumulative income share is greater for **x** than for **y**, resulting in the **x** curve lying completely above the **y** curve, a situation where **x** Lorenz dominates **y**. Based on this pattern, it is conclusive that **x** is less unequal than **y**. This conclusion would still hold if $L_x(p) = L_y(p)$ for some, but not all, values of p.

Lorenz intersection arises when $L_x(p) > L_y(p)$ at some ps and $L_x(p) > L_y(p)$ at other ps, as shown in Figure 4.2. When the Lorenz curve for **x**={0.4, 99.9, 99.9, 99.9, 99.9} and that for **y**={60, 60, 60, 60, 160} intersect, an alternative criterion is needed for deciding which distribution is less unequal. Thus, Lorenz dominance and intersection summarize two broad types of patterns of the difference in the inequality between two distributions.

For small-size populations, it is easy to show graphically whether Lorenz dominance holds between two distributions. When the population sizes are

60

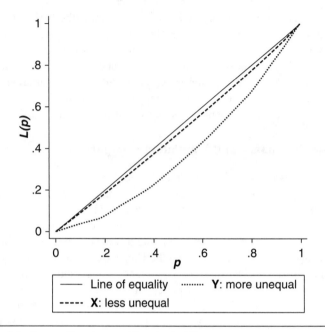

Figure 4.1   Lorenz Dominance: Hypothetical Data

large, for example, an actual income distribution of a country, a state, or a city, we usually select a limited number of ps for graphical views, for it is impractical to view the differences at all ps. Thus, using summary inequality measures becomes necessary. These measures must be *Lorenz consistent* in the first place.

Lorenz consistency is a combination of satisfying three out of the five principles we discussed above: the weak principle of transfers, the scale invariance principle, and the principle of population. An inequality measure is said to be Lorenz consistent if the Lorenz domination of **y** by **x** implies that the inequality measure for **x** is at most that of **y**. On the other hand, if a Lorenz-consistent inequality measure is greater for **x** than for **y**, we cannot conclude that **x** Lorenz dominates **y**. This statement requires that all Lorenz-consistent inequality measures must *unanimously* show that **x** is less unequal than **y**, which is termed the unanimity ordering among Lorenz consistent inequality measures (Shorrocks & Slottje, 2002). Given the large number of Lorenz-consistent inequality measures (expanded by the wide range of parameters such as θ for the generalized entropy family and ε for the Atkinson family), examining all Lorenz-consistent inequality measures is not practical.

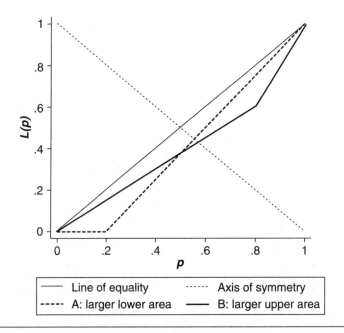

Figure 4.2 Lorenz Intersection: Hypothetical Data

The unanimity ordering requirement becomes even more impractical when we compare more than two distributions. The number of pairwise comparisons grows geometrically with the number of distributions.[2] And we need to examine all Lorenz-consistent inequality measures in each of these pairwise comparisons. It would be highly appealing if we could identify a few inequality indexes that can predict Lorenz dominance with a high level of accuracy.

In searching for a solution, we need to better understand why using different Lorenz-consistent inequality measures may give different results about the Lorenz dominance of two distributions. The heart of the problem is that different measures are sensitive to income differences in various parts of the distribution. For example, the Gini coefficient and the Theil index are middle sensitive and the bottom fifth share is bottom sensitive. In contrast, a generalized entropy with a large positive parameter θ is sensitive in the top extreme tail, whereas a generalized entropy with a large negative parameter is sensitive in the bottom extreme tail. It is possible that a collection of three indexes, each of which is sensitive to the middle region, the lower extreme or the higher extreme, will predict the unanimity ordering with a high level of accuracy.

Based on their study of the income distributions of 80 countries (3,160 pairwise comparisons) using 100 Lorenz-consistent inequality measures, Shorrocks and Slottje (2002) identify three such inequality measures. These indexes target different regions of a distribution. GE_{10} (the generalized entropy at $\theta = 10$) targets the top extreme tail; GE_{-20} (the generalized entropy at $\theta = -20$) targets the bottom extreme tail, and the below-median share $L_{(0.5)}$ targets the lower half of the distribution. The patterns produced by these three indexes match 99% of the patterns yielded by using 100 inequality measures. None of the other combinations of a few inequality measures, neither a range of the same type such as the Atkinson family with different ε nor a combination of the Gini coefficient and others, can predict unanimity with a similar level of accuracy.

Here we see how the flexibility of generalized entropy facilitates inequality comparisons and the usefulness of extreme values of θ (10 and -20) beyond the usual range $[-1,2]$ discussed in Chapter 3. In addition, we see the importance of not relying on a single inequality measure, while many researchers are still using the Gini coefficient exclusively. Classical works from Kolm (1969) to Atkinson (1970) to Sen (1973) warn us against relying on a single inequality measure. A use of just a few different inequality measures as suggested by Shorrocks and Slottje (2002) can effectively and accurately compare inequality across populations or over time.

Shorrocks and Slottje's (2002) three inequality measures may not exactly apply to all empirical work. However, paying attention to the middle to lower region and the two extremes of a distribution can serve as a guiding principle. We use the SIPP income trend data and compare the income distributions in 8 years (28 pairwise comparisons), using five Lorenz consistent inequality measures: the three used in Shorrocks and Slottje (the lower 50% population's income share $L_{(0.5)}$ and two generalized entropy measures tapping the two extremes of the distribution GE_{-20} and GE_{10}) plus the Theil index T and the Gini coefficient G. Table 4.4 shows these five inequality measures for the 8 years examined. Column 1 for the income share owned by the lower 50% of the population ranks 1993 as the least unequal (the largest share) and 1996 the most unequal (the smallest share), which is similar but not exactly the same as what the Theil index and Gini coefficient indicate (1995 the least unequal and 1996 the most unequal). The two measures tapping the extremes also rank the years different from each other and from the measures focusing on the middle and lower regions. When focusing on the bottom extreme, 1988 is ranked the most unequal and 1987 the least. When focusing on the top extreme, 1996 is ranked the most unequal and the 1995 the least. We perform 28 pairwise comparisons using each of the five inequality measures. The unanimity ordering emerging from these results reveals that the U.S. income distribution in 1991 is more unequal than that in 1993. We state that the 1993 income distribution Lorenz dominates the 1991 income distribution. However, no certain conclusion can be made for other years. Although we use five inequality measures, this conclusion can be reached by using only the three suggested by Shorrocks and Slottje (2002).

Year	$L_{(0.5)}$	T	G	E_{-20}	E_{10}
1985	0.23104	0.24678	0.38580	1.34E+65	60,908
1987	0.22846	0.25165	0.38986	2.03E+55	1,414
1988	0.23360	0.23588	0.37962	1.73E+83	467
1991	0.23316	0.23985	0.38132	1.42E+70	5,336
1993	0.23464	0.23395	0.37859	3.05E+70	1,214
1995	0.23441	0.23287	0.37781	4.67E+63	428
1996	0.21001	0.31931	0.42486	6.46E+73	8,857,682
2001	0.21078	0.30725	0.42206	1.36E+81	281,443

Table 4.4 Inequality Measures Tapping the Middle Portion and Two Extremes: Income Trends

Note: Results are based on 8 years of Survey of Income and Program Participation (SIPP) data.

Summary

This chapter, together with Chapter 3, has focused attention on a set of widely used inequality measures, from those related to probability distributions to those based on quantile functions and Lorenz curves, and from those derived from social welfare functions to those developed from information theory. The five principles for summary inequality measures facilitate choices for inequality measures for examining a population's distribution. Lorenz dominance provides a guideline for using a minimum set of inequality measures for comparing population distributions. This approach to population comparisons is to obtain summary inequality measures from *a single* distribution first and then compare these summary measures across populations. An alternative approach is to make a relative distribution based on two distributions first and then look at the summary inequality measures of this relative distribution. This is the topic of the next chapter.

Appendix

Table 4.A1 Properties of Inequality Measures

Inequality Measures	Principle of Transfer	Scale Invariance	Principle of Population	Additive Decomposability	Range (0,1)
Relative to probability distribution					
Range R	Fail	No	Yes	No	No
Variance V	Strong	No	Yes	Yes	No
Coefficient of variation c	Weak	Yes	Yes	Yes	No
Log variance v	Fail	Yes	Yes	No	No
Variance of logs v_1	Fail	Yes	Yes	No	No
Based on quantile functions and Lorenz					
Quantile ratio	Fail	No	Yes	No	No
Quantile interval share	Fail	Yes	Yes	No	No
Gini coefficient G	Weak	Yes	Yes	No	Yes
Derived from social welfare function					
Atkinson index A_ε	Weak	Yes	Yes	No	Yes
Developed from information theory					
Generalized entropy GE_θ	Strong	Yes	Yes	Yes	No

CHAPTER 5. RELATIVE DISTRIBUTION METHODS

Thus far, in comparing two distributions, the approach adopted has been to compare summary statistics for each, or in the case of Lorenz dominance, determine whether the entire Lorenz curve for one distribution exceeds that of the other. The relative distribution method allows for a more thorough comparison of distributions, by creating a single relative distribution aimed at describing how one distribution relates to the other. One advantage of the relative distribution method is that it can be applied to distributions without restrictions on their ranges. For instance, one can consider relative distributions when negative values are possible. In addition, the relative distribution defines a unitless measure, enabling one to compare relative distributions for different pairs of populations corresponding to various quantities one might wish to measure, for example, income, years of education, height, and weight. Several inequality measures can be derived immediately from the relative distribution. Another key advantage is that the relative distribution method allows for separate examination of specific portions of distributions, in particular, the lower and upper tails. Handcock and Morris (1999) provide a systematic introduction to the relative distribution method for social science audiences, and this chapter draws basic materials from that source. For empirical researchers, we supply formulas that can be applied to the sample data. The objective of this chapter is to present the relative distribution method as an important complement to existing summary inequality measures.

Relative Rank, Relative Distribution, Relative Density

The relative distribution concept can be introduced whenever the distribution of some quantity across two populations is to be compared. To proceed, it is necessary to single out one of the two distributions, refer to it as the comparison distribution, and refer to the other as the reference distribution. For example, when we compare income in the black population with that of the white population, we would typically use the black income distribution as the comparison and the white income distribution as the reference, since the black population is the minority population.

The relative distribution notion depends crucially on the idea of determining for any individual value y in the comparison population, its *rank* relative to the reference distribution. This *relative rank* is defined as the proportion of the reference population whose values are at most y. Letting F^0 denote the cumulative distribution function (CDF) for the reference population, this proportion is given by $F^0(y)$. In this context, the transformation that determines relative ranks of such y values in the reference population is referred to as the *grade transformation*, and when data for the comparison population are transformed by this grade transformation, the resulting data are referred to as *relative data*. A user-written module "relrank" by Jann (2008) is available in Stata to perform the grade transformation and create the relative data.

To illustrate, consider the relative rank of the black median income ($26,763) in the white income distribution. We look for the cumulative probability below this value in the white income distribution, that is, the proportion of white households having income less than $26,763, which happens to be 0.2975. Thus, the grade transformation applied to the median black income value is $r = F^0(\$26,763) = 0.2975$, which shows that a typical black household (at the median black income) ranks lower than one third in the white distribution.

Let Y denote a random value drawn from the comparison distribution. The *relative distribution* is defined as the distribution of the relative rank of this (random) value. We use R to denote this random relative rank, so that $R = F^0(Y)$, the grade transformation of a random draw from the comparison distribution. Immediately from the definition, we see that R takes values between 0 and 1. The quantity R can be interpreted as the relative position in the reference population of a random draw from the comparison population, where, by relative position, we mean the proportion of the reference population whose value is at or below the value for the random draw.

We use the notation F for the CDF of the comparison distribution (black income), $Q = F^{-1}$ for the corresponding quantile function, and we let Y denote a random variable having F as its CDF (e.g., Y is a sampled black income). Analogously, F^0, Q^0, and Y^0 denote these quantities for the reference population (whites). As a random variable, R has a CDF, referred to as the relative CDF, which we denote by G; a probability density function (the relative PDF), which we denote by g; and a quantile function, defined as the inverse of the relative CDF; that is, $Q_R(r) = G^{-1}(r)$. By definition, the relative CDF gives the probability that R is less than or equal to a given value r, so we can express this in terms of the comparison CDF and the reference quantile function:

$$G(r) = P[R \leq r] = P[F^0(Y) \leq r] = P[Y \leq Q^0(r)] = F(Q^0(r)).$$

In other words, the relative CDF G is equivalent to $F \circ Q^0$, which is the function defined by $(F \circ Q^0)(r) = F(Q^0(r))$, and which is referred to as the composition of the two functions F and Q^0.

The quantile function for the relative distribution can be derived by inverting the relative CDF

$$(F \circ Q^0)^{-1} = (Q^0)^{-1} \circ F^{-1} = F^0 \circ Q,$$

so the quantile function takes the form $Q_R(r) = F^0(Q(r))$. Observe that if we reverse the roles of the comparison and reference distributions, so that the relative CDF $\tilde{G}$ becomes the CDF of the random variable $\tilde{R} = F(Y^0)$, then we see that

$$\tilde{G}(r) = P[\tilde{R} \le r] = P[F(Y^0) \le r] = P[Y^0 \le Q(r)] = F^0(Q(r)),$$

the original relative quantile function; that is, the reversal makes the CDF equal to the original quantile function, and the quantile function becomes the original CDF.

The relative CDF has a simple interpretation: As with any CDF, it allows one to determine where a distribution is concentrated, in this case, where the comparison distribution's quantiles are concentrated relative to those of the reference distribution. It is a monotonically increasing function satisfying $G(0) = 0$ and $G(1) = 1$. The graph of the function is contained in the unit square: $\{(r, s) : 0 \le r \le 1, 0 \le s \le 1\}$ and extends from the lower-left-hand corner $(0, 0)$ to the upper-right-hand corner $(1, 1)$. An appearance of this function as a straight line with a slope of 1 (so that $G(r) = r$ for all values of the variable r) corresponds to the case when the two distributions are identical.

Other extreme cases allow for immediate interpretation. If the relative CDF takes the value 0 for values of r less than some particular value r^* and then exhibits a jump of size 1 at r^*, and takes the value 1 for values of r greater than r^*, we know that all individuals in the comparison population have values equal to the r^*th quantile of the reference population. More generally, the relative CDF could be any discrete probability distribution concentrated in the unit interval $[0, 1]$, in which case, its graph would appear flat except for k jumps of sizes $p_1, p_2, \ldots, p_k$ at points $r_1, r_2, \ldots, r_k$ in $[0, 1]$. This situation would correspond to one in which the comparison distribution is concentrated on the kth quantiles of the reference distribution $Q^0(r_1), \ldots, Q^0(r_k)$ with proportions $p_1, p_2, \ldots, p_k$. As noted in the introduction, the relative distribution is unitless. Knowing the relative distribution reveals no information about the actual *values* of the quantiles of either the comparison or reference population. The relative distribution merely provides a mapping between the two distributions in the sense that it allows one to determine which quantile from one distribution corresponds to a given quantile from the other.

Returning to the example above, we can take r to be 0.2975, so that as noted, the rth quantile of the reference (white) income distribution is \$26,763. On the other hand, \$26,763 is the median of the comparison (black) income distribution, so as a consequence, we can reinterpret the grade transformation observation above as a statement about the relative CDF at the particular value of 0.2975:

$$G(0.2975) = F(\$26,763) = \frac{1}{2}.$$

A similar calculation can be carried out for every value of r between 0 and 1, which results in a rather comprehensive summary of the relationship between the two income distributions.

The calculation just illustrated is carried out in a straightforward two-step manner to yield the empirical relative CDF based on data collected for the two populations. First, we determine an (empirical) quantile function for the reference distribution. Letting the reference data be denoted by $y_1^0, \ldots, y_n^0$, we order these values from smallest to largest to produce the order statistics $y_{(1)}^0, \ldots, y_{(n)}^0$. We define the empirical quantile function at values of r of the form $k/(n+1)$ by taking $\hat{Q}^0(k/(n+1)) = y_{(k)}^0$. For r between successive values, say $k/(n+1)$ and $(k+1)/(n+1)$, we define $\hat{Q}(r)$ by linear interpolation, taking

$$\hat{Q}^0(r) = \frac{r - (k/(n+1))}{1/(n+1)} y_{(k+1)}^0 + \frac{((k+1)/(n+1)) - r}{1/(n+1)} y_{(k)}^0.$$

Next, we make use of the comparison sample $y_1, \ldots, y_{n'}$ to complete the calculation of the empirical relative CDF. For any given value of r, we take

$$\hat{G}(r) = \frac{\text{No. of } \{y_i \le \hat{Q}^0(r)\}}{n'}$$

the proportion of values in the comparison sample, $y_1, \ldots, y_{n'}$ less than or equal to $\hat{Q}^0(r)$.

Additional qualitative statements about the relationship between the two distributions can be gleaned from the relative CDF. The graph of the relative CDF falling entirely below the diagonal, that is, $G(r) \le r$ for all r (see Figure 5.1a), corresponds to the condition that $Q^0(r) \le Q(r)$ for all values of r, meaning that no reference distribution quantile exceeds the corresponding comparison distribution's quantile; for example, the 25th percentile in the reference population is less than or equal to the 25th percentile in the comparison population, the 50th percentile in the reference population is less than or equal to the 50th percentile in the comparison population, the 75th percentile in the reference population is less than or equal to the 75th percentile of the comparison population, and so on, a very strong sense in which the comparison population is better-off than the reference population. On the other hand, the graph of the relative CDF lying entirely above the diagonal $G(r) \ge r$ for all r (see Figure 5.1b) would correspond to the condition that $Q^0(r) \ge Q(r)$ for all values of r, meaning that no comparison population quantile exceeds the corresponding reference distribution's quantile. If the relative CDF has an inverted S-shape with $G(1/2) = 1/2$ (see Figure 5.1c), this would correspond to the case when those in the lower quantiles of the comparison population are worse-off than those in the corresponding reference population and those in the upper quantiles of the comparison population are better-off than those in the corresponding reference population.

The relative distribution has the attractive property of invariance with respect to monotone transformations. Given a monotone increasing function ψ, if we apply this function to the values in both the reference and the comparison populations, the relative CDF is unchanged. For example, if we apply a log transformation to all incomes in both populations, the relative

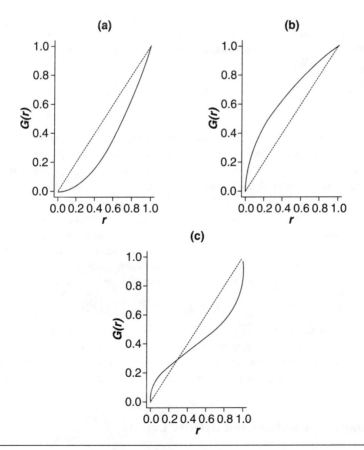

Figure 5.1   Three Scenarios of Relative CDF

distribution is unaffected. As a consequence, any summary statistic derived from the relative distribution will have this invariance property. To see that the property holds, observe that the CDF of $\psi(Y)$, the transformed comparison value Y, becomes

$$P[\psi(Y) \leq x] = P[Y \leq \psi^{-1}(x)] = F(\psi^{-1}(x)),$$

making the CDF the composition function $F \circ \psi^{-1}$, and the quantile function for $\psi(Y)$ becomes the composition $\left(F \circ \psi^{-1}\right)^{-1} = \psi \circ F^{-1} = \psi \circ Q$. Similarly, the CDF and quantile function of $\psi(Y^0)$, the transformed reference value Y^0, are given by $F^0 \circ \psi^{-1}$ and $\psi \circ Q^0$, respectively. It follows that the relative CDF under the transformation becomes the composition

$$(F \circ \psi) \circ (\psi^{-1} \circ Q^0) = F \circ Q^0,$$

which is the same as the relative CDF before the transformation.

Summary statistics for the relative distribution can be used to contrast a comparison and a reference distribution. For example, the mean of the relative distribution,

$$E(R) = \int_{r=0}^{1} rg(r)dr = E[F^0(Y)] = \int_{y=-\infty}^{\infty} F^0(y)f(y)dy,$$

gives the expected proportion of the reference population whose value falls below that of a randomly drawn value from the comparison distribution. For pairs of identical distributions, this value would be ½, so it is quite natural to compare the mean of the relative distribution to ½. When $E[R] < 1/2$, less than half of the reference population will, on average, have a value below that of a randomly drawn value from the comparison population, so on average a majority will have larger values. Roughly speaking, we can think of the comparison population as having lower values than the reference population. When $E[R] > 1/2$, we can draw the opposite conclusions.

Similarly, the median of the relative distribution,

$$G(1/2) = F(Q^0(1/2)) = P[Y \leq Q^0(1/2)],$$

is given by the proportion of the comparison population whose value falls below the median of the reference population. Thus, the condition $G(1/2) < 1/2$ shows a tendency for the reference population to have smaller values than the comparison population, and again, if $G(1/2) > 1/2$, we reach the opposite conclusion.

Relative Proportions and Relative Density

The relative PDF is also easy to interpret as it describes where individuals at various quantiles in the comparison distribution are concentrated in terms of the quantiles of the reference distribution. As for any PDF, the total area under the curve is one, and the function at a point is simply the derivative of the relative CDF there. The area under the curve between two values r_1 and r_2 is the proportion of the comparison population whose values lie between the r_1th and r_2th quantiles of the reference population.

Differentiating the expression for the relative CDF $G(r) = F(Q^0(r))$ with respect to r yields an expression for the relative density function:

$$g(r) = \frac{f(Q^0(r))}{f^0(Q^0(r))}. \tag{5.1}$$

Given data sampled from the two populations: $Y_1^0, ..., Y_m^0$ from the reference population and $Y_1, ..., Y_n$ from the comparison population, the most intuitive approach to relative density estimation is based on *relative proportions*. We pick a number of values at which to calculate quantiles; in the following discussion, we use deciles. We use the reference data to calculate reference sample deciles $\hat{Q}^0(i/10)$. Then we compute the proportion p_i of the comparison sample lying in each tenth $J_i = [\hat{Q}^0(i/10), \hat{Q}^0((i+1)/10))$. The piecewise constant function whose value on the interval J_i is p_i can be viewed as a simple estimator of the relative density. Assuming that the comparison and reference distributions are the same, we expect this function to look approximately like the uniform density in [0, 1], that is, we expect the value to be approximately 1 over the entire interval. Deviations from this baseline situation are easily interpreted.

More sophisticated methods for estimating the relative density are readily available. In fact, estimating the relative density $g(r)$ from data is considerably more subtle than estimation of the relative CDF G, since, as is apparent from examination of Expression 5.1, determining the PDF at a value r involves estimation of the PDF of both the reference and comparison distributions from data at the reference distribution quantile $Q^0(r)$. Consequently, to appreciate the issues involved, one need only consider the problem of estimating the PDF of a distribution based on a sample from it. The following is a brief discussion of kernel density estimation aimed at alerting readers who are unfamiliar with density estimation to some key issues.

Consider a sample $X_1, ..., X_n$ from a distribution F with PDF f. Since $f(x)$ is the derivative of F at x, we can write

$$f(x) = F'(x) = \lim_{\Delta \to 0} \frac{F(x + \Delta) - F(x - \Delta)}{2\Delta},$$

and we can estimate $f(x)$ by picking a small value of Δ and taking

$$\hat{f}(x) = \frac{\hat{F}(x + \Delta) - \hat{F}(x - \Delta)}{2\Delta}, \tag{5.2}$$

where $\hat{F}(x)$ denotes the empirical CDF based on the sample, that is,

$$\hat{F}(x) = \frac{\text{No. of } X_i \leq x}{n}.$$

The numerator in Equation 5.2 is then the number of data points X_i that fall within the interval $[x - \Delta, x + \Delta]$, and the density estimate is the proportion of points per unit length near x.

Two key insights lead to improved density estimation. First, the simple density estimator just described can be expressed in the form

$$\frac{1}{n\Delta} \sum_{i=1}^{n} \phi\left(\frac{x - X_i}{\Delta}\right),$$

where ϕ is the function defined by

$$\phi(u) = \begin{cases} 1/2 & \text{if } |u| \leq 1 \\ 0 & \text{otherwise} \end{cases},$$

the uniform PDF in the interval $[-1, 1]$. Such a density estimator is referred to as a kernel density estimator with kernel ϕ. In this case, the kernel is rectangular shaped. However, it is now understood that if we replace this function by a smooth probability density that is symmetric about 0, we can gain considerable efficiency. Second, the choice of the constant Δ, referred to as the *bandwidth* of the estimator, turns out to be crucial; choosing too small a value leads to an estimator with low bias and a high variance, while choosing too large a value leads to an estimator with a low variance but a high bias. Much statistical research has been focused on the problem of choosing an optimal bandwidth, one that minimizes a combination of bias and variance. (A Stata module "reldist" by Jann, 2008, provides a number of kernel density methods to estimate the relative PDF.) A discussion of the various approaches is beyond the scope of this book. Still, it is important for readers to be aware that methodology for relative density estimation relies heavily on these basic ideas.

To illustrate relative distribution methods, we use relative proportions based on our Stata codes applied to the same example of black income and white income. First, we rank the income data within blacks and whites. The deciles divide the white population into 10 equal-sized ranges (see the first two columns of Table 5.1). For example, the poorest 10% of whites have income lower than \$12,580 and the richest 10% have at least \$103,098. There are 10 decile ranges: the minimum to \$12,580, \$12,580 to \$19,828, until \$103,098 to the maximum of the white income. Ten percent of whites fall in each of the 10 decile ranges. We then determine the proportions of blacks over the ranges defined by the white deciles (see Column 3). The white deciles correspond to quite different quantiles in the black income distribution: The first white decile corresponds to the 0.234 black quantile and the ninth white decile corresponds to the 0.968 black quantile. This means that the poorest 23.4% blacks have income lower than $12,580, and 3.1% of blacks (1 − 0.969) have at least $103,098. Now we are ready to calculate the proportion ratios over the white decile ranges.

We obtain the white proportions and black proportions from their respective quantile ranges, shown in Columns 4 and 5. Then we take the ratio of a black proportion to the corresponding white proportion to get the relative proportion (see Column 6). The relative proportion declines from 2.341 over the first range to 0.311 over the highest range.

Figure 5.2a shows the white income and black income density functions, which clearly have different central locations and shapes. Figure 5.2b draws the black-to-white relative proportions over the corresponding decile ranges. As stated above, we view the plotted curve as an approximation to the relative density, and we see that this relative density curve is downsloping, with a steeper decline below $r = .4$ than above.

Decomposition of Relative Density

In Chapter 2, we introduced the idea of location, scale, and shape of a distribution. Using the reference distribution as the base, the comparison distribution can be conceived as obtained by applying a series of operations to the reference distribution: First apply a location shift, then a scale shift, and finally a shape shift. Study of the relative distribution amounts to using the quantile of the reference distribution as the preferred unit of measurement. The relative density decomposition makes use of this idea to describe the effect of these three operations.

In our black-white income difference example, a pure location shift can be described in relative density terms by taking the white income distribution as the reference, making the location-adjusted white income the comparison distribution. This location adjustment reduces every white household's income by the same amount (e.g., the black-white mean income gap) to yield identical *centers* of the distributions, maintaining the shapes of the two distributions. Beyond a pure location shift, the two distributions can differ by shape, which is captured by comparing the black income with the location-adjusted white income. One can further decompose the shape shift into a scale shift followed by a shape shift.

We illustrate a simple two-component decomposition that describes a comparison distribution as obtained from the reference by a location shift followed by a scale/shape shift. First, we create a location-adjusted reference

White Income Decile (y_r)	Cumulative Proportion		Proportion		Relative Proportion
	White	Black	White	Black	Black Versus White
Minimum	0.0	0.000	—	—	—
12,580	0.1	0.234	0.1	0.234	2.341
19,828	0.2	0.384	0.1	0.150	1.498
26,952	0.3	0.504	0.1	0.120	1.204
34,199	0.4	0.601	0.1	0.097	0.969
42,165	0.5	0.697	0.1	0.096	0.958
51,720	0.6	0.780	0.1	0.083	0.831
62,983	0.7	0.855	0.1	0.075	0.746
78,067	0.8	0.914	0.1	0.059	0.590
103,098	0.9	0.969	0.1	0.055	0.549
Maximum	1.0	1.000	0.1	0.031	0.311

Table 5.1 Black-White Relative Proportion: SIPP 2001

Note: SIPP, Survey of Income and Program Participation.

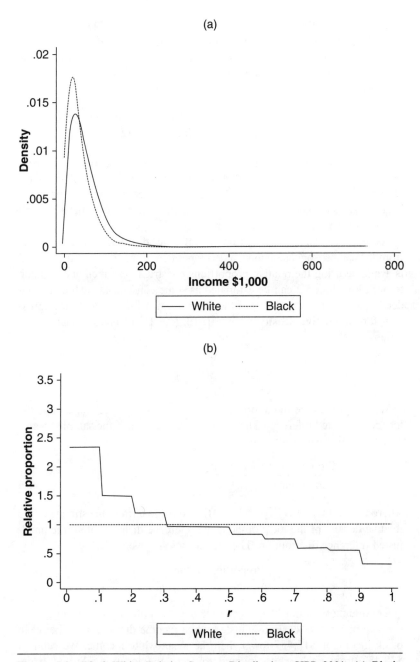

Figure 5.2   Black-White Relative Income Distribution, SIPP 2001: (a) Black-White Income Density and (b) Black-White Relative Proportion

random variable Y^{0L} with the density function f^{0L} and the CDF F^{0L}. Let μ_Y and μ_Y^0 be the mean of Y and Y^{0L}, so that the mean-adjusted reference variable is $Y^{0L} = Y^0 + (\mu_Y - \mu_Y^0)$, while the shapes of the two distributions remain the same. Algebraically, we can express the relative density of the comparison distribution (5.1) as

$$g(r) = \frac{f(Q^0(r))}{f^0(Q^0(r))} = \frac{f^{0L}(Q^0(r))}{f^0(Q^0(r))} \times \frac{f(Q^0(r))}{f^{0L}(Q^0(r))}. \tag{5.3}$$

In words, the overall relative density is the location shift relative density multiplied by an expression that describes the additional shape shift required to make the two distributions match up after the reference has been location shifted. Note that all relative densities reference to the same rth quantile of the reference distribution $Q^0(r)$.

For empirical data, $y_1^0, ..., y_m^0$ from the reference distribution, and $y_1, ..., y_n$ from the comparison distribution, a decomposition of the form in Equation 5.2 is available using the relative proportions construct described above. Each term in Equation 5.2 can be estimated as some constant in each estimated decile range $[i/10, (i + 1)/10)$ of the reference distribution, and the expression for the relative density for r in $[i/10, (i + 1)/10)$ is a product of two ratios:

$$\hat{g}(r) = \frac{\hat{f}^{0L}}{\hat{f}^0} \times \frac{\hat{f}}{\hat{f}^{0L}}. \tag{5.3'}$$

We introduce the notation $y_i^{0L} = y_i^0 + (\bar{y} - \bar{y}^0), i = 1, ..., m$ for the location-adjusted reference data, so that $\bar{y}$ and $\bar{y}^0$ denote the sample means. The first ratio term is given by

$$\frac{\text{Proportion of } y_i^{0L} \text{ in } J_i}{\text{Proportion of } y_i^0 \text{ in } J_i} = 10 \times \text{number of } y_i^{0L} \text{ in } J_i,$$

where $J_i = [\hat{Q}^0(i/10), \hat{Q}^0((i + 1)/10))$. This ratio term is an estimate of the relative density of the location-adjusted reference distribution to the unadjusted reference distribution. The second ratio is given by

$$\frac{\text{Proportion of } y_i \text{ in } J_i}{\text{Proportion of } y_i^{0L} \text{ in } J_i}.$$

Continuing with our black-white income example, we use mean adjustment to obtain the location-adjusted white income distribution. The mean black income is $18,457 lower than the mean white income. We subtract $18,457 from each white income to form the location-adjusted white income, which has the same mean as the black income distribution but retains the scale and shape of the original white income distribution. The relative proportion of the location-adjusted white income to original white income is obtained in the same manner as for the overall relative proportion. Note that the relative proportions of the black income to the location-adjusted white income reference the quantiles for the original unadjusted white distribution. We illustrate this procedure in Table 5.2. The first column lists the original white deciles (same as the first column of Table 5.1). Column 2 shows that the quantile ranges for the location-adjusted white income corresponding to the original white income decile ranges are no longer equal sized. The result for black income density over the original white income decile ranges is the same as that in Table 5.1. The relative proportion for blacks versus location-adjusted whites is shown in the last column of the table.

Figure 5.3a shows the relative densities of location-adjusted white income to white income, capturing the location shift. It indicates a high concentration of location-adjusted whites at the lower end. We interpret this as saying that the black-white location difference is responsible for placing disproportionately more blacks in the lower tail of the income distribution. Figure 5.3b shows the relative densities of black income to location-adjusted white income, capturing the shape shift. The relative proportions of shape shift are lower at the two ends and higher over the second to fifth decile ranges. This reveals that the black-white scale/shape shift contributes to allocating more blacks in the lower-middle income brackets.

With these two relative proportions, we are ready to decompose the overall relative proportion, shown in Table 5.3. Over each quantile range, the overall relative proportion is the product of (1) the relative proportion of the location-adjusted white income to the original white income and (2) the relative proportion of the black income to the location-adjusted white income.

The same idea extends in a natural way to allow for a three-component decomposition of the overall relative density. We can successively decompose the component for the shape shift into scale shift and beyond-scale shape shift. Let f^{0LS} be PDF for the location-scale-adjusted reference distribution. Equation 5.1 can be expanded sequentially as follows:

$$g(r) = \frac{f(Q^0(r))}{f^0(Q^0(r))} = \frac{f^{0L}(Q^0(r))}{f^0(Q^0(r))} \times \frac{f^{0LS}(Q^0(r))}{f^{0L}(Q^0(r))} \times \frac{f(Q^0(r))}{f^{0LS}(Q^0(r))}. \quad (5.4)$$

In words, the overall relative density is a product of the location shift relative density, a density ratio term that describes a scale shift, and a density ratio term that accounts for the effect that remains after location and scale effects have been accounted for. The decomposition is a sequential

White Income Decile (y_r)	Cumulative Proportion		Proportion		Relative Proportion
	Location-Adjusted White	Black	Location-Adjusted White	Black	Black Versus Location-Adjusted White
Minimum	0.000	0.000	—	—	—
12,580	0.358	0.234	0.358	0.234	0.654
19,828	0.451	0.384	0.093	0.150	1.604
26,952	0.535	0.504	0.084	0.120	1.434
34,199	0.610	0.601	0.075	0.097	1.294
42,165	0.680	0.697	0.070	0.096	1.366
51,720	0.751	0.780	0.071	0.083	1.172
62,983	0.818	0.855	0.067	0.075	1.115
78,067	0.881	0.914	0.063	0.059	0.944
103,098	0.935	0.969	0.054	0.055	1.013
Maximum	1.000	1.000	0.065	0.031	0.479

Table 5.2 Relative Proportion for Black Versus Location-Adjusted White: SIPP 2001

Note: SIPP, Survey of Income and Program Participation.

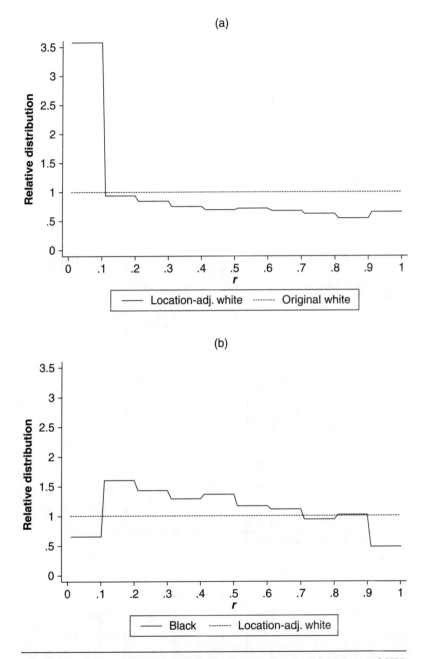

Figure 5.3 Decomposing Relative Distribution, Black and White Income of SIPP 2001: (a) Location-Shift Relative Proportion and (b) Shape-Shift Relative Proportion

1	2	3	4	5	6
Cumulative Proportion for Original Whites	Original White Income Decile	Overall RP	Location Shift	Shape Shift	(4) × (5)
0.0	Minimum	2.341	3.579	0.654	2.341
0.1	12,580	1.498	0.934	1.604	1.498
0.2	19,828	1.204	0.840	1.434	1.204
0.3	26,952	0.969	0.749	1.294	0.969
0.4	34,199	0.958	0.701	1.366	0.958
0.5	42,165	0.831	0.710	1.172	0.831
0.6	51,720	0.746	0.669	1.115	0.746
0.7	62,983	0.590	0.625	0.944	0.590
0.8	78,067	0.549	0.542	1.013	0.549
0.9	103,098	0.311	0.650	0.479	0.311
1.0	Maximum	—	—	—	—

Table 5.3 Sequential Decomposition of Overall Relative Proportions (RP) Into Location and Shape Shifts: SIPP 2001

Note: SIPP, Survey of Income and Program Participation.

one, as terms are included in succession, with each new term accounting for an additional modification to a distribution. The decomposition obtained depends critically on the order in which terms are introduced. If, for example, we first adjusted for scale, and then for location, the result would be completely different decomposition. Also, it should be noted again that every density term has as its argument the rth quantile of the original reference distribution, and only the first ratio in the decomposition is a relative density since the argument to the densities in that term are the quantiles of the denominator PDF.

As for the previous decomposition (Equation 5.3'), we can use data to arrive at a decomposition of the relative proportions into products of relative proportion terms, each of which results from a particular type of modification:

$$\hat{g}(r) = \frac{\hat{f}}{\hat{f}_0} = \frac{\hat{f}^{0L}}{\hat{f}^0} \times \frac{\hat{f}^{0LS}}{\hat{f}^{0L}} \times \frac{\hat{f}}{\hat{f}^{0LS}}. \qquad (5.4')$$

In the three-component decomposition, we need to compute ratios of counts, just as we did for the two-component decomposition, except now we have terms involving location as well as scale adjustment. The terms appearing in Equation 5.4' that appear in the two-term decomposition are calculated as before, while the last two terms on the right-hand side in Equation 5.4' are obtained as illustrated in Table 5.2. The counts in the numerator of the second term of (5.4') are location- and scale-adjusted white incomes. For these, we multiply each white's income by the ratio of the black standard deviation to the white standard deviation and then adjust the mean difference. For example, letting s_y and s_y^0 denote the standard deviations of the comparison and reference data, the location-scale-adjusted reference data become

$$y_i^{0LS} = \frac{s_y}{s_y^0} y_i^0 + (\bar{y} - \bar{y}^0).$$

Then the second relative proportion term takes the form

$$\frac{\text{Proportion of } y_i^{0LS} \text{ in } J_i}{\text{Proportion of } y_i^{0L} \text{ in } J_i}.$$

Continuing with our black-white income example, Table 5.4 shows the sequential three-component decomposition, first location shift (Column 4), then scale shift (Column 5), and finally beyond-scale shape shift (Column 6). Figure 5.4 provides the graphic view of scale shift and shape shift after the location shift is taken out. Figure 5.4a shows that the scale for the black income is narrower than that for the white income, concentrating on the range from the second decile to the seventh decile. Figure 5.4b shows that once the scale difference is factored out, black income is more polarized than the white income as more blacks are in two ends of the location-scale-adjusted distribution.

While the density ratios and the decompositions provide us with tools for comparing two distributions, and for understanding sources of differences between these distributions, there are two particular summary measures available for succinct characterization of differences. We proceed to discuss relative entropy and median relative polarization (MRP) in the next section.

Summary Measures of Relative Distribution

Measures that summarize relative densities will facilitate precise answers to many of our research questions. For example, what is the degree of divergence between black and white income distributions? How is the comparison distribution polarized as compared with the reference distribution? Relative entropy and MRP can be used to answer these questions.

Relative Entropy

In Chapter 3, we introduced various measures of inequality for distributions, such as the Theil index, and generalized entropy measures. These quantities measure the intrinsic degree of inequality for a single distribution. An alternative approach is to measure inequality relative to a reference distribution. To this end, we introduce the notion of *relative entropy*. Given comparison and reference distributions with a positive relative PDF g, the relative entropy is defined to be

$$\int_{r=0}^{1} g(r) \log(g(r)) dr. \tag{5.5}$$

There is clear similarity in this expression with the definition of entropy. However, viewing this expression as a measure of entropy is somewhat misleading. For one thing, given the definition of entropy in the discrete case, we should expect a minus sign in Equation 5.5, so this quantity measures something that is the opposite of entropy. Even if we correct the sign in Equation 5.5, there remain key technical problems with extending the entropy concept to the continuous case in the manner when we approximate continuous distributions by discrete ones, as the natural limiting operation we are inclined to carry out leads to ignoring a term that tends to infinity as we let bin sizes reduce to zero.

A better way to interpret Expression 5.5 is using the notion of *Kullback-Leibler divergence* of one distribution from another, a notion that we motivate

	1	2	3	4	5	6	7
	Cumulative Proportion for Original Whites	Original White Income Decile	Overall RP	Location Shift	Scale Shift	Residual Shape Shift	$(4) \times (5) \times (6)$
	0.0	Minimum	2.341	3.579	0.534	1.226	2.341
	0.1	12,580	1.498	0.934	1.665	0.964	1.498
	0.2	19,828	1.204	0.840	1.677	0.855	1.204
	0.3	26,952	0.969	0.749	1.565	0.827	0.969
	0.4	34,199	0.958	0.701	1.496	0.913	0.958
	0.5	42,165	0.831	0.710	1.341	0.874	0.831
	0.6	51,720	0.746	0.669	1.107	1.007	0.746
	0.7	62,983	0.590	0.625	0.847	1.115	0.590
	0.8	78,067	0.549	0.542	0.681	1.488	0.549
	0.9	103,098	0.311	0.650	0.483	0.991	0.311
	1.0	Maximum	—	—	—	—	—

Table 5.4 Sequential Decomposition of Overall Relative Proportions (RP) Into Location, Scale, and Residual Shape Shifts: SIPP 2001

Note: SIPP, Survey of Income and Program Participation.

83

84

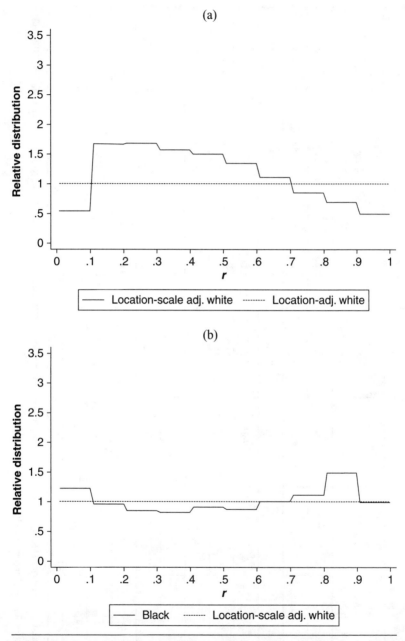

Figure 5.4 Sequential Decomposition of Overall Relative Distribution Into Location, Scale and Residual Shape Shifts, Black and White Income of SIPP 2001: (a) Scale-Shift Relative Proportion and (b) Beyond-Scale Shape-Shift Relative Proportion

as follows. Suppose we have a sample of observations $Y_1, \ldots, Y_n$, and we wish to test the null hypothesis that the sample is drawn from a distribution P with PDF p against the alternative that the sample is drawn from a distribution Q with PDF q. The Neyman-Pearson Lemma (Neyman & Pearson, 1933) tells us that the most powerful test at any prescribed level α is a likelihood ratio test that rejects the null hypothesis if the log-likelihood

$$\log \Lambda = \log\left(\frac{\prod_{i=1}^{n} q(Y_i)}{\prod_{i=1}^{n} p(Y_i)}\right) = \sum_{i=1}^{n} \log\left(\frac{q(Y_i)}{p(Y_i)}\right)$$

exceeds some constant c_α depending on α. The log-likelihood is a sum of independent and identically distributed random variables, so assuming the alternative hypothesis is true, we can use the strong law of large numbers to write

$$\frac{\log \Lambda}{n} \approx E_q\left[\log\left(\frac{q(X)}{p(X)}\right)\right] = \int_{x=-\infty}^{\infty} \log\left(\frac{q(x)}{p(x)}\right) q(x)dx,$$

as the sample size tends to infinity. When q differs from p, we expect the likelihood ratio to take values typically greater than 1. The degree to which this value exceeds 1 is therefore measured by the last integral, which is referred to as the Kullback-Leibler divergence of P from Q, denoted by $D(P,Q)$ (Kullback & Leibler, 1951; Soofi, 1994). It can be shown that this quantity is nonnegative and takes the value zero if and only if the two distributions coincide. We think of the Kullback-Leibler divergence as measuring how far P is from Q. However, some care is required in interpreting this as a *distance* since, for example, it is not generally the case that $D(P;Q) = D(Q;P)$.

Returning to the relative entropy (5.5), we rewrite it using Expression 5.1 in the form

$$\int_{r=0}^{1} \frac{f(Q_0(r))}{f_0(Q_0(r))} \log\left(\frac{f(Q_0(r))}{f_0(Q_0(r))}\right) dr$$

making a change of variables $y = Q_0(r)$, so that $r = F_0(y)$ and $dr = f_0(y)dy$; this expression takes the form

$$\int_{y=-\infty}^{\infty} \frac{f(y)}{f_0(y)} \log\left(\frac{f(y)}{f_0(y)}\right) f_0(y)dy = D(F_0; F),$$

the Kullback-Leibler divergence of F_0 from F.

Expressing the relative entropy in terms of relative proportions over decile ranges is straightforward. We can write (5.5′)

$$D(F : F^0) = \sum_{k=1}^{10} \left(\frac{P_k}{P_k^0}\right) \log\left(\frac{P_k}{P_k^0}\right) P_k^0.$$

Continuing with our black and white income example, we use (5.5′) to calculate the overall relative entropy as 0.137 in 2001.

Relative entropy has an important drawback that goes back to an invariance under reordering property of entropy. Two different relative distributions will have the same relative entropy if one is obtained from the other by *shuffling* the probability mass. To be more precise, if g is a relative density, and $\tilde{g}(r) = g(h(r))$ for some *measure-preserving*[1] function $h:[0, 1] \rightarrow [0, 1]$, then $\tilde{g}$ and g have the same relative entropy. So, for example, consider the case when g is constant in each decile range, say g takes the value g_i in the ith decile range $[(i-1)/10, i/10)$, for $i = 1, \ldots, 10$, and $\tilde{g}$ takes the same values, but in different decile ranges, so that the decile ranges are reordered, then the relative entropies of $\tilde{g}$ and g remain the same. Consequently, the actual *location* of peaks and valleys in the relative density has no bearing on its relative entropy.

Relative Polarization

A distribution is described as polarized if there is a tendency to concentrate in the tails rather than the middle. Polarization is another way to characterize the scale/shape of a distribution, and this characterization can be comparative. We often ask whether a comparison distribution stretches wider (narrower) or has heavier (lighter) ends than the reference distribution. For example, we wish to know, as compared with the white income distribution, is the black income distribution less stretched and clustering in the lower half (i.e., more convergent toward the median of the distribution)? The relative entropy does not offer an answer to this question.

The MRP index is a measurement of the degree to which a comparison distribution is more polarized than a reference distribution. It is defined in terms of the relative distribution of the comparison distribution relative to the location-adjusted reference distribution, where the reference distribution is median-adjusted so that the medians of the two distributions are identical. (Median adjustment is preferred to mean adjustment because of drawbacks of the mean when distributions are skewed.) We use the notation R_{0L} for a random variable whose distribution is the relative distribution between the comparison distribution and the location-adjusted reference distribution. This random variable can be interpreted as the proportion of the location-adjusted reference distribution lying at or below a random draw from the comparison distribution. We then measure how far, on average, R_{0L} deviates from ½ in absolute value and

---

[1] A general measure-preserving transformation can be thought of as a transformation defined by cutting up the unit interval [0,1] into any number of pieces, then shuffling the pieces.

define the relative polarization and as a linear transformation of that average by taking

$$\text{MRP}(F; F^0) = 4E[|R_{0L} - 1/2|] - 1. \tag{5.6}$$

The choice of the linear transformation (four times the expected deviation minus 1) results in an index taking values between −1 and 1. Consideration of some important special cases enhances the interpretability of this index. If, after location adjustment, the two distributions coincide, then as noted before, R_{0L} has a uniform distribution in the interval [0, 1], and in this case, $E[|R_{0L} - 1/2|] = 1/4$, making the MRP index equal to 0. The most extreme case of lack of relative polarization is one in which the comparison population is concentrated at the median of the reference. In this case, R_{0L} is a constant random variable taking the value of ½, so that $E[|R_{0L} - 1/2|] = 0$, making the MRP equal to −1. Finally, the most extreme case of relative polarization is the one in which half of the comparison population has a value equal to the minimum of the reference population, while the other half has a value equal to the maximum of the reference. In this case, R_{0L} will take the value of 0 with probability ½ and 1 with probability ½ making $|R_{0L} - 1/2|$ a constant random variable equal to ½. In this case, $E[|R_{0L} - 1/2|] = 1/2$, and we see that MRP takes the value of 1.

An MRP greater than 0 indicates that the comparison group is more polarized than the reference group, whereas an MRP less than 0 indicates that the comparison is less polarized than the reference group. Thus, the MRP provides information on both the direction and magnitude of difference on upper and lower portions of the distributions being compared.

The value of the MRP index can be interpreted as a proportional shift of the population from more central location to less central locations. For example, the MRP for black-white income comparison is −0.2299 meaning that 22.99% of the black households converge toward the median in comparison with white households. This appears to reflect the wider income scale for whites than for blacks.

Calculation of the MRP based on data can be described as follows. Let m and m^0 denote the sample medians for the comparison and the reference, respectively. The median-adjusted reference data become $\tilde{y}_i^0 = y_i^0 + (m - m^0)$, for $i = 1, \ldots, n$. We use the *empirical* grade transformation to convert these values to relative *median-adjusted* data $\tilde{r}_i = \tilde{F}^0(y_i)$, the proportion of median-adjusted reference data points less than or equal to y_i, for $i = 1, \ldots, n$ and take the sample MRP to be

$$\text{MRP} = \frac{4}{n} \left(\sum_{i=1}^{n_y} |\tilde{r}_i - 1/2| \right) - 1. \tag{5.6'}$$

The MRP index has additional notable properties. In particular, it is anti-symmetric, meaning that swapping the comparison and reference will yield an index of the same magnitude and opposite sign. To see this, consider Figure 5.5, which gives a plot of an example of $G(r)$ for some choice of comparison and reference distributions whose medians are identical. The fact that the medians are identical guarantees that the graph of the function passes through the point $(1/2, 1/2)$ in the center of the unit square. If we take r to be a uniformly distributed random variable in the interval $[0, 1]$, then the distribution of $Q(r)$ is that of a random variable Y sampled from the comparison distribution, and $F^0(Q(r))$ has the distribution of the random variable R. Consequently, we can write

$$E|R - 1/2| = \int_{r=0}^{1} |F^0(Q(r)) - 1/2| dr.$$

This integral is represented in the figure as the area filled with vertical stripes. On the other hand, if we swap the reference and comparison distributions, as observed before, we obtain a random variable $\tilde{R}$ whose distribution is the new relative distribution, and whose CDF is the inverse of the CDF of R. It follows that $E|\tilde{R} - 1/2|$ is the area filled with horizontal stripes. Clearly, the sum of these two areas is ½. So we can write,

$$E|R - 1/2| + E|\tilde{R} - 1/2| = 1/2.$$

It follows that

$$(4E|R - 1/2| - 1) + (4E|\tilde{R} - 1/2| - 1) = 4(1/2) - 2 = 0;$$

that is, the sum of the two MRP indices is 0, or in other words, $\text{MRP}(F; F^0) = -\text{MRP}(F^0; F)$.

One possible drawback of the MRP is that alone it does not reveal which tail of the distribution is the source of polarization. To address this, the MRP can be decomposed into the lower- and higher-portion polarizations. This requires separating the calculation for the lower half and upper half of the location-adjusted relative distribution. In the example referred to in Figure 5.5, this amounts to using the fraction of the lower-left-hand square with horizontal stripes to calculate the lower-portion relative polarization (LRP) and the fraction in the upper-right-hand square to calculate the upper-portion relative polarization (URP). Then the MRP can be additively decomposed into the LRP and URP:

$$\text{MRP}(F; F^0) = \frac{1}{2}\text{LRP}(F; F^0) + \frac{1}{2}\text{URP}(F; F^0). \tag{5.7}$$

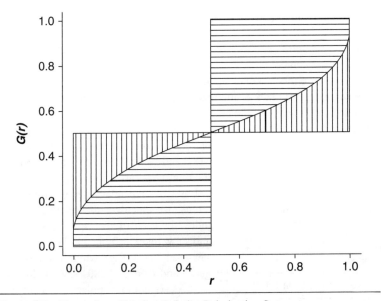

Figure 5.5 Illustration of Median Relative Polarization Symmetry

In terms of data, after sorting the median-adjusted relative data in an ascending order, the LRP and the URP can be calculated as follows:

$$\text{LRP}(F; F^0) = \frac{8}{n} \left(\sum_{i=1}^{n/2} (1/2 - \tilde{r}_i) \right) - 1,$$

$$\text{URP}(F; F^0) = \frac{8}{n} \left(\sum_{i=n/2+1}^{n} (\tilde{r}_i - 1/2) \right) - 1. \qquad (5.7')$$

We use "reldist" (Jann, 2008) to obtain these polarization measures. In comparing black income and white income in 2001, we find that the MRP is not evenly distributed in the two tails. The LRP = −0.3152 is twice as negative as the URP = −0.1447. Thus, the lower half of the black households have narrower spread than the white lower half. About 16% (half the LRP) of blacks in the lower half converge toward the median. The upper half of black households are more similar to the white households with only about 7% converging toward the median. Taken together, we can see that the black distribution is more right skewed than the white distribution.

Trends of Relative Distributions

Relative distribution methods create relative data that offer greater flexibility in analyzing inequality. For instance, we are interested in knowing how the black-white income distributional differences evolve over time. Do we see a stagnation of black-white income differences after the progress made in the 1970s? We can use the black-white relative density and the sequential decomposition to provide graphic views. We can use the relative entropy to understand the overall divergence and MRP and its decomposition to understand the relative polarization.

Based on the relative proportions over tenths, we calculate the relative entropy index for each of the eight survey years and show them in Table 5.5. The year 1987 saw the highest black-white income divergence and 1996 and 2001 saw the lowest.

Next, we compare polarization between the black and white distributions. Like the single-year illustration in Table 5.5, we use the median adjustment and obtain the median, lower-tail, and upper-tail relative polarization indexes using reldist (Jann, 2008). Because the comparison focuses on the shape difference after adjusting for the median, the relative polarization summarizes the scale shift and the shape shift. The relative polarization offers information on the magnitude and direction of differences between black and white distributional tails, which are not revealed in the relative entropy. The results are shown in Table 5.6 and Figure 5.6. The most salient pattern is that the MRP and LRP fluctuate, whereas the URP remains relatively unchanged over time. Figure 5.6 shows visually the stability of URP and the fluctuation of the LRP, which contributes to the fluctuation of the MRP, the overall relative polarization.

Year	Relative Entropy
1985	0.184
1987	0.241
1988	0.180
1991	0.199
1993	0.170
1995	0.166
1996	0.140
2001	0.137

Table 5.5 Relative Entropy: Trends of Black-White Income Divergence From 1985 to 2001, SIPP

Note: SIPP, Survey of Income and Program Participation.

How do the relative distribution decomposition methods differ from summary inequality measure decompositions, such as the Gini decomposition introduced in Chapter 4? We stress the many opportunities offered by the relative distribution approach that combines two distributions. The relative distribution methods are flexible in summarizing the divergence and

Year	MRP	LRP	URP
1985	−0.2321	−0.3112	−0.1529
1987	−0.2547	−0.3648	−0.1445
1988	−0.2060	−0.2907	−0.1214
1991	−0.2407	−0.3408	−0.1407
1993	−0.2145	−0.3003	−0.1286
1995	−0.2195	−0.3217	−0.1173
1996	−0.2429	−0.3708	−0.1150
2001	−0.2299	−0.3152	−0.1447

Table 5.6 Median Relative Polarization (MRP) and the Lower and Upper Components: Trends of Black-White Income Polarization From 1985 to 2001, SIPP

Note: MRP = 0.5(LRP + URP). LRP, lower-portion relative polarization; SIPP, Survey of Income and Program Participation; URP, upper-portion relative polarization.

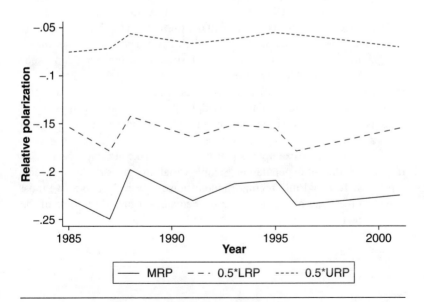

Figure 5.6 Trends of Black-White Income Median and Lower and Upper Relative Polarization From 1985 to 2001, SIPP

polarization of two distributions. These quantities are useful for both cross-sectional and time trend studies, providing alternative measures of inequality that complement the existing summary inequality measures. For instance, the greater relative entropy indicates greater inequality between the comparison and reference groups. The polarization indexes provide measures sensitive to both lower and upper tail, whereas summary inequality measures are sensitive to one tail—either bottom or top.

With these findings, we are in a good position to answer the two questions we raised in the beginning of the chapter. During the 17 years from 1985 to 2001, black-white income divergence fluctuates, which is mainly due to the fluctuation of the lower half of the black income distribution.

Summary

How do the relative distribution decomposition methods differ from summary inequality measure decomposition introduced in Chapter 4? We have presented opportunities offered by the relative distribution approach that combines two distributions. The relative distribution methods are flexible in dissecting the overall difference into location and scale and shape shifts. The relative entropy is different from Theil's index and other generalized entropy indexes discussed in earlier chapters primarily because the relative entropy characterizes divergence of two distributions. The MRP and its LRP and URP components are particularly useful because they compare the shape, with an emphasis on the two tails, of two distributions, net of the median influence. We have provided illustrations using population subgroups (blacks vs. whites). However, the application of relative distribution methods in general, and MRP in particular, can be wide. We can directly apply these relative-distribution-based methods to spatial comparisons, such as cross-regions within the United States or cross-national comparisons, as well as comparisons over time.

All the illustrative examples so far in this book take the empirical data as if they were the entire population. Sample variability gives rise to imprecise estimates. To avoid interpreting random noise as a real pattern, we must attend to the issue of the inference of inequality measures, a topic of the next chapter.

CHAPTER 6. INFERENCE ISSUES

In many research situations, only sample data are available rather than the whole population. Furthermore, national survey data are collected from surveys using complex sampling designs such as multistage cluster, stratified sampling, so that often, if not always, individuals in the population have different probabilities of being sampled. As a result, the inferences for inequality measures for the response variable (standard errors and confidence intervals) are subject to sampling variability that is more complicated than for simple random sampling. Furthermore, since virtually all summary inequality measures are nonlinear functions of the outcome variable, a linearization method is used to derive the standard error, which is more complicated, while incorporating the survey sampling design. Finally, when the sample size is small, the linearization method and its asymptotic assumption may be questionable, calling for alternative approaches to quantifying sampling variability. These issues are discussed in this chapter.

Inequality measures, particularly the Gini coefficient, the Theil index, and the Atkinson family, are widely used in trend studies (e.g., comparing income inequality over time), comparative studies (e.g., comparing income inequality across countries), and policy studies (e.g., comparing the redistributive effects of various taxing policies). When making such comparisons, statistical significance becomes an important issue that is often ignored. This chapter deals with inference issues related to inequality measures and relative distribution measures.

Broadly speaking, two approaches—asymptotic and bootstrap—are used to handle inference for inequality measures. The asymptotic approach is based on normal approximation to the sampling distribution. Asymptotic standard errors (ASEs) and confidence intervals based on asymptotic theory may be biased in small samples, and the small sample properties of these estimates are typically unknown. The bootstrap approach estimates the sampling distribution using 500 to 2,000 bootstrap samples from the actual sample. The bootstrap inferential statistics, including bootstrap standard error (BSE) and confidence intervals, can be applied to relatively smaller samples because it does not make the asymptotic assumption (Burr, 1994; Hall, 1992). Simple random sampling is assumed for both approaches, so both need to be adapted to complex survey sampling design situations.

A general guideline for choosing an approach can be drawn from Duclos and Araar (2006). When the number of observations is large and the sampling distribution of the estimator for summary inequality measures tends to be normal, we can safely use an asymptotic approach, which produces practically the same results as the bootstrap approach. However, if the sampling distribution of the estimator is far from normal, the asymptotic approach produces biased standard errors and confidence intervals.

This chapter introduces both asymptotic and bootstrap approaches to summary inequality measures from a single distribution or a relative distribution. These approaches can take into account survey sampling designs. We will provide empirical examples using the Survey of Income and Program Participation (SIPP) data on income and wealth for illustration.

The Asymptotic Approach With Survey Design Effect

Duclos and Araar's (2006) book provides a Stata program to perform the estimation of the Gini coefficient, the Atkinson family, the generalized entropy family, quantile ratios, and share ratios and their ASEs and confidence intervals, taking into account survey sampling designs. We review a few basics from their work before applying the method to empirical examples.

According to Duclos and Araar (2006), under the law of large numbers and the central limit theorem, it is possible to show that most of the inequality measures mentioned above are consistent and asymptotically normally distributed. Consistency says that as the sample size goes to infinity, the estimator approaches the true population parameter. Asymptotic normality says that for large samples, the sampling distribution of the estimator is approximately normal. The authors use a standard *linearization* approach to derive the standard errors of these inequality measures. This approach guarantees that a linear approximation to a given inequality measure has a distribution that is approximately normal with mean given approximately by the true population measure and some variance that can be consistently estimated from the data.

Complex survey sampling designs can affect the precision of the standard error of inequality measures. National representative surveys in the United States typically use multistage cluster, stratified sampling designs. Clusters—for example, metropolitan statistical areas (MSAs)—are more heterogeneous among population elements within clusters than between clusters. On the other hand, strata are more homogeneous within than between. Cluster sampling amounts to selecting clusters for inclusion using a weighted sampling scheme, whereas stratified sampling typically involves the inclusion of all strata. For example, for a study of racial differences in income, MSAs might be stratified by the percentage of residents who are black; MSAs with a large percentage of blacks can be oversampled so that more black respondents are included in the final sample than would otherwise be obtained.

Selecting only some clusters leads to a sample that is not as diverse as the population, and this is something that needs to be accounted for in estimating variances of inequality measures. Similarly, randomly selecting elements within strata differs fundamentally from simple random sampling, and this sampling design must be accounted for as well. The multistage cluster and stratified sampling designs sometimes give rise to unequal probability of selection among population elements. The inverse of a probability of selection is the sampling weight, representing the number of population elements represented by a sampled element. Inequality measures are meant to summarize properties at the population level, but failing to take into account sampling weights produces a description of the sample only. Thus, sampling weights must be used to correct for bias.

We use SIPP data to illustrate a complex sampling design. The SIPP uses a stratified and two-stage cluster sampling design. Strata are formed by grouping small counties within regions (Northeast, Midwest, South, and West) based on a variety of demographic and socioeconomic variables. In the first stage of the cluster sampling, the primary sampling units (PSUs) are clusters (counties, independent cities, and county groups). A sample of PSUs is drawn from each stratum of county groups, while all large counties and independent cities are included. In the second stage, households are selected from each selected PSU. The PSU and strata variables in the public-use SIPP are quasi measures to avoid potential identification of small geographic areas and sampled individuals. In the public-use SIPP, the number of strata is 73 and the number of PSU is 144 for the SIPP 1991 data. The corresponding numbers are 105 and 210 for the SIPP 2001 data. The stratified and cluster sampling leads to different sampling weights for selected households. In addition, not all sampled households were willing to participate, and not all of those participants in the first wave could be followed up. The nonresponse rate and lost-to-follow-up (attrition) rate also contribute to the final sampling weights for selected households.

A program, DASP (Distributive Analysis Stata Program; Duclos & Araar, 2006), is freely available for obtaining asymptotic inference for both single-inequality measures and the difference in an inequality measure between two populations. DASP, which can be easily installed in Stata, has the capacity to provide ASEs that account for survey sampling designs for most of the standard inequality measures.

The two sections in Table 6.1 show estimates of income inequality measures. The top section shows the unweighted estimates with the standard errors and confidence intervals that assume simple random sampling. The bottom section shows the weighted estimates with the standard errors and confidence intervals that properly take into account the complex survey sampling design and aim to correct for bias to be expected in the top section. For example, the unweighted Gini is 0.423, greater than the weighted Gini (0.422). The upward bias of the unweighted estimate holds for all measures that are middle or top sensitive. On the other hand, the unweighted bottom-sensitive measures, $p10/p50$, GE_{-1} and A_2 are downwardly biased and the bias is more substantial than that in the middle- or top-sensitive inequality measures.

Standard error estimates in the top section will also tend to be biased since simple random sampling is assumed. We need to incorporate information about the survey design, including the cluster sampling information (PSU) and the stratified sampling information (STRATA). Using an asymptotic method appropriate for the survey design in DASP, the bottom section of Table 6.1 shows larger standard error and wider confidence interval estimates than those in the top section. For example, the 95% confidence interval is [0.420, 0.427] for Gini under the simple random sampling assumption. After the sampling design is taken into account, the 95% confidence interval becomes [0.417, 0.427]. The sampling variability discrepancy appears to be smaller for middle-sensitive measures and greater for bottom- or top-sensitive measures, particularly GE_{-1}.

Interest in inequality measures is not limited to the analysis of single populations. We are also interested in making comparisons between populations. In comparing two populations, we often wish to test the null hypothesis that the difference in an inequality measure between two populations is 0, a task DASP allows. We consider the example of comparing income inequality in the United States between 1991 and 2001. Table 6.2 shows the point estimate, standard error, t ratio, p value, and 95% confidence interval for the same set of inequality measures examined in Table 6.1 for household income in 1991, 2001, and their difference (the 2001 value minus the 1991 value). The evidence is strong that income inequality is significantly greater in 2001 than in 1991. Despite the mean income (in constant dollar terms) increase from $48,065 in 1991 to $51,250 in 2001, the income of the lower half of the population is stagnant as shown by the insignificant change in $p10/p50$ quantile ratio. In contrast, the upper half grew disproportionately: the $p90/p50$ ratio increased from 2.29 to 2.49, and the change is significant. This divergence led to the significant growth of all other inequality measures over the 10 years. For example, the bottom-sensitive GE_{-1} grew from 1.3741 to 3.8592 and the top-sensitive GE_2 increased from 0.2677 to 0.4041, with a milder growth in middle-sensitive measures such as the Gini (from 0.3823 to 0.4216).

How do group income differences contribute to the total income inequality? The additive decomposability principle discussed in Chapter 4 suggests that the generalized entropy family satisfies this principle. Table 6.3 shows

Measure	Estimate	SE	95% Confidence Interval	
Unweighted without survey design				
Gini	0.423	0.002	0.420	0.427
$p10/p50$	0.281	0.003	0.275	0.288
$p90/p50$	2.510	0.019	2.473	2.547
GE_{-1}	3.512	0.766	2.010	5.014
GE_0	0.349	0.004	0.342	0.356
GE_1	0.310	0.004	0.303	0.317
GE_2	0.405	0.009	0.388	0.422
$A_{(1/2)}$	0.149	0.001	0.147	0.152
A_1	0.294	0.002	0.289	0.299
A_2	0.875	0.024	0.829	0.922
Weighted with survey design				
Gini	0.422	0.003	0.417	0.427
$p10/p50$	0.287	0.004	0.280	0.294
$p90/p50$	2.494	0.023	2.449	2.540
GE_{-1}	3.859	0.893	2.090	5.629
GE_0	0.346	0.004	0.337	0.354
GE_1	0.308	0.005	0.299	0.317
GE_2	0.404	0.010	0.384	0.425
$A_{(1/2)}$	0.148	0.002	0.145	0.152
A_1	0.292	0.003	0.286	0.298
A_2	0.885	0.024	0.839	0.932

Table 6.1 Estimates and Inferences of Income Inequality Measures: SIPP 2001
Note: SIPP, Survey of Income and Program Participation.

Measure	Estimate	SE	t	p > t	95% Confidence Interval	
Gini_91	0.3823	0.0023	164.6	0.000	0.3776	0.3869
Gini_01	0.4216	0.0025	169.6	0.000	0.4167	0.4265
Difference	0.0393	0.0034	11.6	0.000	0.0326	0.0460
$p10/p50\_91$	0.2904	0.0051	56.4	0.000	0.2801	0.3007
$p10/p50\_01$	0.2865	0.0035	81.5	0.000	0.2795	0.2935
Difference	−0.0039	0.0062	−0.6	0.533	−0.0162	0.0084
$p90/p50\_91$	2.2941	0.0222	103.3	0.000	2.2498	2.3383
$p90/p50\_01$	2.4943	0.0228	109.5	0.000	2.4492	2.5395
Difference	0.2002	0.0318	6.3	0.000	0.1375	0.2630
GE_{-1}_91	1.3741	0.3124	4.4	0.000	0.7513	1.9969
GE_{-1}_01	3.8592	0.8925	4.3	0.000	2.0896	5.6288
Difference	2.4851	0.9456	2.6	0.010	0.6191	4.3511
GE_{0}_91	0.2851	0.0042	67.7	0.000	0.2767	0.2935
GE_{0}_01	0.3457	0.0043	80.4	0.000	0.3371	0.3542
Difference	0.0606	0.0060	10.1	0.000	0.0487	0.0725
GE_{1}_91	0.2407	0.0031	78.7	0.000	0.2346	0.2468
GE_{1}_01	0.3078	0.0045	68.8	0.000	0.2989	0.3166
Difference	0.0671	0.0054	12.4	0.000	0.0564	0.0778
GE_{2}_91	0.2677	0.0044	61.1	0.000	0.2590	0.2764
GE_{2}_01	0.4041	0.0104	39.0	0.000	0.3835	0.4246
Difference	0.1364	0.0112	12.1	0.000	0.1142	0.1586
$A_{(1/2)}\_91$	0.1216	0.0015	81.6	0.000	0.1186	0.1245
$A_{(1/2)}\_01$	0.1482	0.0017	85.1	0.000	0.1447	0.1516
Difference	0.0266	0.0023	11.6	0.000	0.0221	0.0311

Measure	Estimate	SE	t	p > t	95% Confidence Interval	
A_1_91	0.2480	0.0032	78.3	0.000	0.2417	0.2544
A_1_01	0.2923	0.0030	96.0	0.000	0.2862	0.2983
Difference	0.0442	0.0044	10.1	0.000	0.0355	0.0529
A_2_91	0.7332	0.0445	16.5	0.000	0.6445	0.8219
A_2_01	0.8853	0.0235	37.7	0.000	0.8387	0.9319
Difference	0.1521	0.0503	3.0	0.003	0.0528	0.2513

Table 6.2 Testing Differences in Income Inequality Measures: SIPP 1991 and 2001
Note: SIPP, Survey of Income and Program Participation.

the decomposition of the Theil index, that is, GE_1, by racial groups and its inferential statistics. Again, we use data on blacks and whites only; thus, the estimate of the population Theil index differs from that in Table 6.2. The total Theil is 0.3052, the between component is the between Theil 0.0081, accounting for 2.7% of the total, and the within component is 0.2971, accounting for 97.3% of the total. The within component is a weighted sum of the group Theil, and the weight is a product of the population share and the group mean to grand mean ratio. The contribution of this weighted group Theil is 0.2669 (87.5% of the total) by whites and 0.03 (9.9% of the total) by blacks. The standard errors are provided for the total and group-specific Theil index, the population share, the group mean to grand mean ratio, and the weighted group-specific contribution, in both absolute and relative terms. All of these statistics are significantly different from zero. Theil's index, a generalized entropy measure when the parameter θ is 1, is middle sensitive. As θ goes up, the contribution of whites goes up, while the contribution of blacks goes down. For GE_2, the relative contribution of whites becomes 91.7% and that of blacks is 6.4%. In the opposite direction, for GE_{-1}, the contribution of whites is lower at 71.7% and that of blacks is higher at 28%.

While income represents the flows of resources of households, wealth represents what is in stock. How did wealth inequality in the United States evolve over the same time period? We examine the difference in inequality measures allowing negative values of net worth between 1991 and 2001 using the SIPP wealth data. The Gini coefficient, quantile-based measures,

Group	Measure	Population Share	$(mu\_k/mu)^\theta$	Absolute Contribution	Relative Contribution
1. Whites	0.2949	0.8633	1.0483	0.2669	0.8746
	0.0047	0.0025	0.0021	0.0044	0.0038
2. Blacks	0.3175	0.1367	0.6950	0.0302	0.0988
	0.0094	0.0025	0.0121	0.0013	0.0046
Within	—	—	—	0.2971	0.9734
	—	—	—	—	—
Between	—	—	—	0.0081	0.0266
	—	—	—	0.0001	—
Population	0.3052	1.0000	—	0.3052	1.0000
	0.0045	0.0000	—	0.0045	0.0000

Table 6.3 Decomposition of Theil's Index for Income by Race: SIPP 2001

Note: SIPP, Survey of Income and Program Participation.

and GE_2 (one half of the squared coefficient of variation) can handle negative and zero net worth. The results are presented in Table 6.4. First, we note that the Gini coefficient for net worth is much greater than that for income. In addition, the Gini increased by 0.069 from 0.6944 in 1991 to 0.7635 in 2001. This increase is significant. The $p25/p75$ ratio declined significantly, indicating a divergence in wealth for the middle 50% of the population. Similarly, the $p50/p95$ ratio declined, suggesting that the typical American household was doing more poorly than the affluent top 5%. We also look at the share ratio of bottom half share to the top 5% share. This share ratio shows how the household wealth had been accrued quickly to the top 5%. Finally, the GE_2, which is ordinally equivalent to the variance and the coefficient of variation, increased tremendously, capturing the very top extremes.

We further examine how racial groups contribute to the total wealth inequality using GE_2 as an example (see Table 6.5). Similar to the decomposition for household income, we look at the black and white subgroups only. The weight for the within component for GE_2 is different from GE_1 (the Theil index) in that we square the group mean to grand mean net worth ratio. Table 6.5 shows that the net worth GE_2 is much higher for whites than for blacks. Only 0.1% of the total GE_2 is contributed by the between-group component while 99.9% is from the within component, of which the diversity of the white race group contributes to 99.8% of the total GE_2, whereas the diversity of the black race group virtually does not contribute to the total GE_2 since the 0.07% is not significantly different from zero.

Using Tables 6.1 to 6.5, we have illustrated the importance of recognizing that the sample is not the population, and of properly accounting for complex survey designs. The inferential statistics, the standard error and confidence interval for single inequality measures, and differences between populations enable us to make conclusions with appropriately quantified degrees of uncertainty.

When the sample size is sufficiently large and the sampling distribution of the estimator becomes approximately normal, the asymptotic approach adjusted for survey designs yields adequate inferential statistics. The DASP program facilitates the asymptotic approach adjusted for survey designs for a variety of inequality measures. For small samples and relative distribution-based inequality measures, it is often suggested that the *bootstrap method* becomes appropriate. The following section introduces this approach. Readers who do not have such a need can skip to the next chapter.

The Bootstrap Approach

Since Efron (1979) and Efron and Tibshirani (1993) popularized the bootstrap approach, it has been increasingly applied to many statistical inference

Index	Estimate	SE	T	p > t	95% Confidence Interval	
Gini_91	0.6944	0.0035	197.5640	0.0000	0.6874	0.7014
Gini_01	0.7635	0.0142	53.8138	0.0000	0.7354	0.7916
Difference	0.0691	0.0146	4.7260	0.0000	0.0402	0.0979
p25/p75_91	0.0378	0.0025	15.0647	0.0000	0.0328	0.0428
p25/p75_01	0.0216	0.0017	12.9010	0.0000	0.0183	0.0250
Difference	−0.0162	0.0030	−5.3537	0.0000	−0.0221	−0.0102
p50/p95_91	0.1014	0.0023	44.0190	0.0000	0.0968	0.1060
p50/p95_01	0.0840	0.0017	49.6032	0.0000	0.0807	0.0874
Difference	−0.0174	0.0029	−6.0757	0.0000	−0.0230	−0.0117
sb50/st5_91	0.1244	0.0052	23.7494	0.0000	0.1140	0.1349
sb50/st5_01	0.0449	0.0120	3.7496	0.0003	0.0212	0.0687
Difference	−0.0795	0.0131	−6.0798	0.0000	−0.1053	−0.0537
GE_2_91	1.4758	0.0635	23.2430	0.0000	1.3492	1.6023
GE_2_01	40.9671	30.0551	1.3631	0.1758	−18.6265	100.5608
Difference	39.4914	30.0551	1.3140	0.1917	−19.8211	98.8039

Table 6.4 Testing Differences in Wealth Inequality Measure Estimates: SIPP 1991 and 2001

Note: SIPP, Survey of Income and Program Participation.

Group	GE_2	Population Share	Square Mean Ratio	Absolute Contribution	Relative Contribution
1. Whites	37.3750	0.8629	1.2553	40.4847	0.9982
	27.1211	0.0025	0.0064	29.5457	0.0013
2. Blacks	3.3032	0.1371	0.0586	0.0266	0.0007
	0.4014	0.0025	0.0067	0.0059	0.0006
Within	—	—	—	40.5113	0.9989
	—	—	—	—	—
Between	—	—	—	0.0456	0.0011
	—	—	—	0.0009	—
Population	40.5569	1.0000	—	40.5569	1.0000
	29.5442	0.0000	—	29.5442	0.0000

Table 6.5 Decomposition of Wealth Inequality Measures by Racial Group: SIPP 2001

Note: SIPP, Survey of Income and Program Participation.

problems. While the ASE is based on an analytical linear asymptotic approximation, the BSE is based on a brute-force computational resampling idea. Below we first briefly introduce the standard bootstrap method (see more details in the QASS volume by Mooney & Duval, 1993). We will also briefly discuss bootstrap methods that take into account survey designs (Duclos & Araar, 2006).

Bootstrap Basics

Starting with a random number seed, we draw B (e.g., 500–2,000) random resamples of size n (or a size smaller than n when n is sufficiently large) with *replacement* from the actual data sample of size n. Each of the bootstrap samples differs slightly from the actual sample and from each other because of sampling with replacement—some observations will appear multiple times in a bootstrap sample and others will be left out. It is also important to note that samples are obtained independently when resampling is carried out. An estimate of the inequality measure of interest is obtained from each bootstrap sample. The resulting 500 to 2,000 estimated inequality measures (e.g., Gini) form a distribution that approximates the sampling distribution of the estimator for Gini. If one wishes to replicate the whole procedure, the same random number seed must be used to get the exactly the same sampling distribution. The bootstrap method follows two steps B times.

1. Take a bootstrap resample of size n with replacement from the actual sample of size n.

2. Calculate the inequality measure of interest using this first bootstrap resample, resulting in B bootstrap estimates, which will be used to calculate bootstrap inferential statistics.

To obtain BSEs, we simply calculate the standard deviation of the bootstrap sample. We usually use $B = 500$ to generate the BSE. We can calculate the 95% confidence interval using 1.96 BSE around the bootstrap mean.

Next, we relax the normality assumption of the sampling distribution of estimates. One method is known as the percentile method. If we have 999 trials and rank the estimated inequality measure (e.g., Gini) from low to high, then the 95% confidence interval is bounded by the 25th and 975th Gini. Because none of the 999 estimated Gini values is out of bounds, the 95% confidence interval will not be out of bound either. We use a larger number of resamples (e.g., 1,000–2,000) to produce the percentile-based confidence interval. Percentile-based confidence intervals perform well in comparison with alternative methods (Burr, 1994).

Several procedures have been developed to address the possibility that the bootstrap distribution of the estimates may be biased, including the *bias-corrected percentile* and the *bias-corrected and accelerated* method (Efron & Tibshirani, 1993; Mooney & Duval, 1993). Here we illustrate the bias-corrected percentile method that involves only the bias correction factor. This method adjusts the lower and upper limits of the interval to the bias in the median (Efron & Tibshirani, 1986):

1. Calculate a bias-correcting factor, which is the standard normal score corresponding to the proportion of bootstrap estimates that are less than the estimate obtained from the actual data. Let $\hat{I}$ be the inequality measure obtained from the actual data, $\hat{I}^*$ be an inequality measure obtained from a bootstrap sample, and z_0 be the bias-correcting factor. We define $z_0 = \Phi^{-1}[\Pr(\hat{I}^* < \hat{I})]$, where Φ is the standard normal CDF, and Φ^{-1} is its inverse function, that is, the quantile (percentile) function. For example, if the proportion of bootstrap estimates lower than the actual estimate is 0.55, the corresponding standard normal score $z_0 = 0.125$.

2. Use this bias-correcting factor to modify the *percentiles* used to calculate the limits of the desired confidence interval: $\text{CI}_{1-\alpha} = [G^{-1}(\Phi(z_{\alpha/2} + 2z_0)), G^{-1}(\Phi(z_{1-\alpha/2} + 2z_0))]$, where $G^{-1}(\cdot)$ is the quantile function of the estimated inequality measures. Essentially, we use different percentiles to adjust for the median bias. For example, for the 95% CI, $z_{\alpha/2} = -1.96$ and $z_{1-\alpha/2} = 1.96$. In the median bias case, we do not use the 25th and 975th bootstrap estimates out of 1,000 repetitions. We correct the z score by adding twice the bias-correcting factor $2z_0 = 2 \times 0.125 = 0.25$. Thus, the bias-corrected z score becomes $-1.96 + 0.25 = -1.71$ for the lower limit and $1.96 + 0.25 = 2.21$. The corresponding cumulative density is 0.044 and 0.986. Thus, the bias-corrected percentile method yields the 95% CI with the 44th bootstrap estimate as the lower limit and the 986th bootstrap estimate as the upper limit.

This bias-correction method assumes that the standard error of the bootstrap estimates is constant for all estimates. When this assumption does not hold, further adjustment is required. Interested readers should read about the acceleration method and bias-correction method in Efron and Tibshirani (1993, p. 186).

Researchers may use a Stata module "ineqerr" by Jolligge and Lrushelnytskyy (1999) to obtain bootstrap inferential statistics for selected inequality measures. "Ineqerr" gives the normality-based, percentile-based, and bias-corrected bootstrap confidence intervals for the Gini coefficient, the Theil index, and the variance of the logarithms.

Using the similar procedure, the bootstrap approach can also be used to test whether the difference in an inequality measure between two populations is significantly different from 0. Based on a resample from both actual samples, we estimate the difference in an inequality between the two samples. These resulting estimated differences approximate the sampling distribution of the difference. See Duclos and Araar (2006).

Bootstrap Inferences for Relative Distribution Measures

Relative distribution methods examine the entire relative distribution of a comparison distribution against a reference distribution, from which summary measures can be obtained. Because the asymptotic properties of estimators for these summary measures are unknown, we take advantage of the robustness of bootstrapped standard error and bootstrapped confidence intervals.

The procedure can be described in four steps:

1. Draw a bootstrap sample from the reference-group sample with replacement and a bootstrap sample from the comparison-group sample with replacement.

2. Based on these two first-round bootstrap samples, we create the bootstrapped relative data, based on which we obtained the first round of summary measures.

3. Repeat Steps 1 and 2 for 1,000 times.

4. The middle 95% of the resulting bootstrap distribution of summary measures defines the 95% confidence interval of the summary measures. The previously discussed bias-correction method can be applied to the bootstrap confidence interval.

In comparing the black income distribution (the comparison) with the white income distribution (the reference), we use the estimates of the relative entropy from 1,000 bootstrap samples to obtain the inferential statistics (see Table 6.6). The observed relative entropy is 0.1375. The 95% percentile-based confidence interval is [0.1204, 0.1576] and the bias-corrected interval is [0.1187, 0.1546]. These results indicate a significant divergence between the black income distribution and the white income distribution. Specifically, the bias-corrected confidence interval shows that the relative entropy has a lower bound of 0.1187 and an upper bound of 0.1546. The median relative polarization (MRP) based on the actual data is estimated as −0.2248, with a 95% confidence interval [−0.2467, −0.2028] and a bias-corrected interval [−0.2475, −0.2033]. The two types of confidence intervals are also provided for lower relative polarization (LRP) and upper relative polarization (URP). This indicates that black income is less polarized than white income, and the LRP accounts for the MRP twice as much as the LRP because the upper limit of LRP (−0.2717 from bias-corrected CI) is much lower than the lower limit of URP (−0.1686).

Bootstrapping With Survey Sampling Designs

When bootstrap sampling is utilized in the context of a complex survey design, we need to take that design into account to produce appropriate standard errors for estimates. Complex survey designs often have clusters (PSUs) and strata from stratifying the sample by characteristics. Compared with simple random sampling, clustering increases standard errors, whereas stratifying decreases standard errors. Complex survey designs usually result in varying sampling weights for the final sampling units. Sampling weights are used to estimate weighted statistics, but it does not help adjust the standard errors of these weighted statistics.

When working with survey data, we should be vigilant about the survey sampling design and extract three essential variables related to the survey design—PSU, Strata, and sampling weights. Because PSU and Strata are geocode sensitive, a usual practice of survey organizations to protect confidentiality is not to provide the actual PSU and Strata. Some surveys provide quasi PSU and Strata that approximate the original design, which is the case for the SIPP data. Bootstrapping from survey data involves drawing bootstrap samples from each stratum (Biewen, 2002; Biewen & Jenkins, 2006; Duclos & Araar, 2006). The "bsample" command in Stata allows

| | | Bootstrap Sample | | | |
| | Actual Sample | Percentile-Based CI | | Bias-Corrected CI | |
Measure	Estimate	25th	975th	25th	975th
RE	0.1375	0.1204	0.1576	0.1187	0.1546
MRP	−0.2248	−0.2467	−0.2028	−0.2475	−0.2033
LRP	−0.3095	−0.3497	−0.2745	−0.3462	−0.2717
URP	−0.1401	−0.1656	−0.1104	−0.1686	−0.1130

Table 6.6. Bootstrap Inferences of Relative Entropy and Relative Polarization Between Black Income and White Income: SIPP 2001

Note: LRP, lower relative polarization; MRP, median relative polarization; RE, relative entropy; SIPP, Survey of Income and Program Participation; URP, upper relative polarization. The bootstrap inferences are based on 1,000 bootstrap samples. MRP = 0.5 × LRP + 0.5 × URP.

survey designs via options that specify Strata and PSU. The software package DAD, a stand-alone distributive analysis package by Duclos and Araar (2006), performs bootstrapping from complex survey data specifically for a set of inequality measures. The Stata module "reldist" by Ben Jann (2008) estimates bootstrapped standard errors from complex survey data for relative polarization and its decomposition. We will show the use of these tools in the final chapter's real-world example.

Performance of the Asymptotic and Bootstrap Approaches

As mentioned above, Duclos and Araar (2006) suggest that when the sample size is large and the sampling distribution of the estimator for summary inequality measures tends to be normal, we can safely use an asymptotic approach. It is unclear what size of a sample is considered sufficiently large. It is also largely unknown whether there are differences in the sampling variability across different types of inequality measures and different regions of a distribution to which an inequality measure is sensitive. To provide answers to these questions, we conducted Monte Carlo experiments treating the SIPP 2001 income data set as if representing an entire population for which we can calculate the "true" value of five inequality measures: Gini (middle-sensitive), Atkinson $A_{1/2}$ (middle-sensitive), Theil (middle-sensitive), GE_{-1} (bottom-sensitive), and GE_2 (top-sensitive). We determine the performance of the two confidence interval techniques using Monte Carlo simulations of the sampling process. We repeatedly draw samples from the population, and treat them as one would if one were to collect sample data and construct a confidence interval for the true inequality measure. By repeating this a large number of times, we are able to determine the performance of the confidence interval technique in terms of the ability to correctly achieve the desired 95% probability of containing the true value (coverage probability) as well as its length and shape.

To compare the asymptotic and bootstrap approaches, we consider two cases: a small sample size (100) and a large sample size (1,000). The objective of the experiment is to evaluate the behavior of the 95% confidence interval using three criteria: (1) the probability for the 95CI to cover the true value (95% is considered a good performance); (2) the average length of the 95CI (the shorter the better); and (3) the shape of the CI represented by the ratio of the upper margin over the lower margin (closer to 1 is desired).

For the asymptotic approach, we draw a sample of either size without replacement, obtain the 95% confidence interval using Dulos and Araar's DASP, and repeat this step 1,000 times. Based on the 1,000 CIs, we obtain summary values for the three criteria. For the bootstrap approach, we draw a sample of either size (100 or 1,000) with replacement and obtain the 95CI using the bootstrap percentile method and the bootstrap bias-corrected and accelerated method (BCa) with 1,000 repetitions. To ensure a fair comparison, the same bootstrap draws were used for the three methods. Again, this step of drawing a sample and constructing a confidence interval is repeated 1,000 times, and we obtain the summary values for the three criteria. Comparing these criteria between the two approaches and across inequality measures leads to the following recommendations. First, the asymptotic approach can be safely recommended if the sample size is 1,000 or more, because the asymptotic approach and the bootstrap approach behave nearly identically and the bootstrap approach requires intense computation time. Second, when the sample size is small, for example, 100, both the asymptotic and bootstrap methods exhibit poor performance. The BCa method improves over the percentile method only slightly. Therefore, we do not recommend the BCa method as a routine practice. Also, there is not much gain associated with the bootstrap approach. In both approaches, the confidence interval, which is based on an estimate of the standard error of the estimator, is narrower than it should be, meaning that the standard error estimate is downward biased. For example, the coverage probability of the 95CI for the Gini coefficient is only about 90% for the small sample case. Third, there are dramatic differences in sampling variability across different types of inequality measures, lower for Gini (more precise) and higher for Atkinson and generalized entropy (less precise). The sampling variability also varies by the region of the distribution to which an inequality measure is sensitive: lowest for the middle sensitive, second lowest for the top sensitive, and very high for the bottom sensitive. In particular, even for a large sample (1,000), the percentage of CIs that cover the true value of GE_{-1} is about 60%, and the coverage is very poor (<20%) when the sample size is 100. Therefore, we must exercise caution when we interpret the inference of bottom-sensitive inequality measures.[1]

Summary

This chapter discusses inferences for inequality measures. We illustrate the computation of the ASE, the confidence interval, and hypothesis testing of a set of inequality measures using DASP that incorporates complex survey designs. We also illustrate the standard bootstrap approach to inferences for relative-distribution-based inequality measures. In addition, we introduce the bootstrap approach to complex survey data. We stress the importance of obtaining inferences for inequality measures so that we can make generalizations to the population with a degree of certainty.

---

[1] The full results of this Monte Carlo experiment can be found at our book Web site.

Up until this point, our focus has been inequality for the whole population or between two populations. Sources of inequality often include more than one grouping variable. Patterns of inequality between two groups confound the effect of a grouping variable with the effects of other factors. To credibly describe the difference between two groups controlling for other factors, we turn to a model-based approach to inequality, the topic of the next chapter.

CHAPTER 7. ANALYZING INEQUALITY TRENDS

Inequality research concerns the uneven distribution of a population's attribute, for example, income. This attribute is associated with some population characteristics, for example, race, education, and age. Between two time periods, there can be changes both in the composition of the population characteristics affecting the attribute marginally and in the conditional distribution of the attribute given these characteristics. Thus, both (1) the change in the composition of characteristics and (2) the change in the distribution of the attribute holding the characteristics constant contribute to the trend of an inequality measure. Here we introduce an approach that decomposes the change in an inequality measure into compositional and conditional components (Machado & Mata, 2005). See related topics on density decomposition in DiNardo et al. (1996) and Jenkins and Van Kerm (2005).

Consider a simple case where the attribute is income and the characteristic is race, with blacks being the minority and whites being the majority. The overall change over time in income inequality is due to two distinctive components—the change in the racial *composition* and the change in the *conditional distribution* of income given race. Combinations of changes in these two components may contribute to the changing inequality in three distinct ways. First, an increase in black-white income gaps and a larger black proportion will unambiguously increase inequality. Second, a decrease in black-white income gaps and a smaller black proportion will unambiguously reduce inequality. Third, an increase (decrease) in black-white income gaps and a smaller (larger) black proportion will lead to an ambiguous overall change in inequality. Thus, it is important to identify each source's contribution. To this end, we use a *counterfactual* decomposition method (Machado & Mata, 2005).

The key element of the counterfactual method is the creation of a counterfactual distribution that does not occur in the real world: the conditional response distribution in one time period given the covariate in another time period. Before we introduce the method, we define the *conditional distribution* as the response distribution given covariates, the *joint distribution* as the distribution of the response and the covariate in conjunction, and the *marginal distribution* as the unconditional distribution, regardless of the covariate. The marginal distribution can be obtained by summing (more generally integrating) the joint probability mass (density) function over all values of the covariates. This procedure for obtaining the marginal distribution based on the joint distribution is called marginalization.

Let y be household income (dropping the household subscript) and let x be a covariate, which can be continuous (e.g., ability) or discrete (e.g., race).

We use C_t to refer to the composition of x at time t. We use $F(y_t; C_t)$ to refer to the marginal distribution of y_t. Note that this is an actual distribution and is not counterfactual. When we consider the composition of the covariate at a different time s, and use the conditional distribution of y at time t, we obtain a counterfactual marginal distribution, which we denote by $F(y_t; C_s)$. The change in a summary inequality measure I from Time 1 to Time 2 is given by $\Delta I = I_2 - I_1 = I[(F(y_2; C_2)] - I[(F(y_1; C_1)]$. By introducing a counterfactual marginal distribution, we can express this change algebraically as follows:

$$\Delta I = \{I[(F(y_2; C_2)] - I[(F(y_2; C_1)]\} \\ + \{I[(F(y_2; C_1)] - I[(F(y_1; C_1)]\}. \tag{7.1}$$

Here, the first term $I[F(y_2; C_2)] - I[F(y_2; C_1)]$ captures the contribution of the change in the covariate composition keeping the conditional distribution fixed; $I[F(y_2; C_1)] - I[F(y_1; C_1)]$ captures the contribution of the change in the conditional response distribution given the covariate, fixing the composition.

In Equation 7.1, the counterfactual inequality fixes the covariate composition at Time 1 and the conditional response distribution at Time 2 $F(y_2; C_1)$. A reverse order is to fix the covariate composition at Time 2 and the conditional response distribution at Time 1 $F(y_1; C_2)$. The decomposition formula becomes $\Delta I = \{I[(F(y_1; C_2)] - I[(F(y_1; C_1)]\} + \{I[(F(y_2; C_2)] - I[(F(y_1; C_2)]\}$. The results between the two orders may differ. We could take their average as the final decomposition.

The counterfactual distribution is easy to understand in the special case when x is dichotomous, taking the value of 0 or 1. In this situation, in any given time period t, there are only two conditional distributions to consider for the attribute y, namely, the distribution of y given $x = 0$ and the distribution of y given $x = 1$. We use $f_t(y|0)$ and $f_t(y|1)$ to denote the conditional probability density function (PDF) or probability mass function (PMF) of y given $x = 0$ or $x = 1$ at time t, and we use $c_t(0)$ and $c_t(1)$ to denote the population proportions with $x = 0$ and $x = 1$, respectively. Then the marginal PDF (PMF) of y (noncounterfactual) at time t is given by

$$f_t(y|0)c_t(0) + f_t(y|1)c_t(1),$$

which takes the form of a weighted average of the two conditional distributions. On the other hand, when we form a counterfactual distribution at time t based on the composition at a different time s, we use the same conditional distributions, but we use the proportion in a different time, replacing the population proportions $c_t(0)$ and $c_t(1)$ with $c_s(0)$ and $c_s(1)$, respectively, to yield

$$f_t(y|0)c_s(0) + f_t(y|1)c_s(1).$$

For the purpose of doing calculations using statistical software, it is useful to view the calculation of inequality measures based on such counterfactual distributions as obtained by using inequality measures with counterfactual sample weights. Defining two weights $w(0) = c_s(0)/c_t(0)$ and $w(1) = c_s(1)/c_t(1)$, we can reexpress the counterfactual at time t as

$$f_t(y|0)c_t(0)\left(\frac{c_s(0)}{c_t(0)}\right) + f_t(y|1)c_s(1)\left(\frac{c_s(1)}{c_t(1)}\right) =$$
$$f_t(y|0)c_t(0)w(0) + f_t(y|1)c_s(1)w(1),$$

which is essentially a weighted marginal distribution at time t. For example, 2,285 blacks and 15,369 whites were sampled in 1991 (time s), and 3,403 blacks and 20,182 whites were sampled in 2001 (time t). For the Order 1 counterfactual, $c_s(1) = 0.1443$ and $c_t(1) = 0.1296$. Then the weights are calculated as $w(1) = 0.1296/0.1443 = 0.8897$ and $w(0) = 0.8704/0.8557 = 1.0076$. For the Order 2 counterfactual, the weights are calculated as $w(1) = 0.1443/0.1296 = 1.1134$ and $w(0) = 0.8557/0.8704 = 0.9831$. These weights should be treated as analytic weights in calculating inequality measures.[1]

This dichotomous case can be generalized to the multicategory case. Suppose there are K categories so that x takes values from $1, \ldots, K$. The population proportion for the kth category is denoted by $c(k)$. The weight for each category is given by

$$w(k) = \frac{c_s(k)}{c_t(k)}.$$

We can use these weights directly to compute weighted inequality measures and test the significance of their differences using DASP (Distributive Analysis Stata Program). In this way, the counterfactual decomposition can be applied to any summary inequality measures. Table 7.1 shows Gini coefficient G, Theil's index T, and generalized entropy GE_2. We average the components between the two counterfactual orderings, which are similar in this example. The results show the overwhelming contribution (97.4–97.9%) of the conditional income distribution given race to the overall inequality change over the decade.

In our example, the conditional income distribution given race can confound with the conditional income distribution given education, and the simple analysis based on race alone is misleading. Typically, we introduce multiple categorical and continuous covariates to better explain the response

---

[1]For analytic weights around 1, Stata internally rescales them to sum to the number of observations in the data. The resulting group proportions are then changed to resemble those in the other year.

Decomposition	G	T	$A_{1/2}$
Actual 1991: $F(y_1; C_1)$	0.381	0.240	0.121
Actual 2001: $F(y_2; C_2)$	0.422	0.307	0.148
Overall change	0.041	0.067	0.027
Counterfactual Order 1: $F(y_2; C_1)$			
Compositional	0.001	0.001	0.001
Conditional	0.040	0.066	0.027
Counterfactual Order 2: $F(y_1; C_2)$			
Compositional	0.001	0.002	0.001
Conditional	0.039	0.066	0.026
Average Counterfactual Orders 1 and 2			
Compositional	0.001	0.001	0.001
Conditional	0.040	0.066	0.026
Percentage contribution			
Compositional	2.5	2.1	2.6
Conditional	97.5	97.9	97.4

Table 7.1 Non-Model-Based Decomposition of Income Inequality: SIPP 1991 and 2001

Note: SIPP, Survey of Income and Program Participation.

variable. The above method does not apply when there are multiple categorical variables or even when just one covariate is continuous. To produce an analysis of trends analogous to what we did above for a single categorical covariate but in these more complex situations, it is necessary to introduce a decomposition that is model based, a model in which we express the distribution of the response variable in terms of the covariates. We now turn to a model-based decomposition method.

The Oaxaca-Blinder regression decomposition method applied to the analysis of the change in wages over two time periods has been widely used (DiNardo et al., 1996; Juhn et al., 1993; Oaxaca, 1973). Using linear regression models, which are conditional mean models, this method decomposes the temporal change in wages into a component capturing the change in the effects of the covariates and a component capturing the change in the composition of the covariates. However, when conditional mean models are fitted, shape changes are absorbed into the residuals. To fully characterize the conditional distribution with both conditional mean and conditional shape, Machado and Mata (2005) extend conditional mean wages to conditional quantile wages using quantile regression. The estimated quantile regression (QR) coefficients are then used together with the composition of the covariates to form the model-based actual and counterfactual marginal wage distributions. Comparing the model-based actual and counterfactual marginal distributions leads to conclusions about the contribution of the composition component and the conditional distribution component. Machado and Mata's distributional method facilitates model-based decomposition of all inequality measures.

As an example, we extend the previous analysis from a single categorical covariate to a vector of covariates, including race, education, age, and the constant term.[2] Henceforth, the notation x_t will be used to refer to such a covariate vector. The quantile regression model (QRM) separately for each time period t can be expressed as follows (see Hao & Naiman, 2007):

$$y_t = \beta_t^p x_t + \varepsilon_t^p,$$

where $0 < p < 1$ indicates the cumulative proportion of the population. Then the pth conditional quantile is a function of y given x in each time:

$$Q_t^p(y_t|x_t) = \beta_t^p x_t.$$

The pth conditional quantile at time t is estimated with the quantile-specific, time-specific parameters, β_t^p, and the values of the covariates x_t.

The model-based decomposition method decomposes the overall changes in the income inequality from Time 1 to Time 2 into the composition of covariates and the conditional distribution of income given the covariates. We construct the model-based marginal distribution through marginalization based on the estimated QR coefficients $\hat{\beta}_t$ and the actual distribution of all covariates C_t:

Model-based marginal: $F(y_t|\hat{\beta}_t; C_t) = (\hat{\beta}_t; C_t)$ for $t = 1, 2$.

The counterfactual marginal distributions are defined as follows:

$$F(y_t|\hat{\beta}_t; C_s) = (\hat{\beta}_t; C_s) \text{ for } t = 1, 2, \ s = 1, 2, \text{ and } t \neq s.$$

As such, the counterfactual distribution represents what income distribution would prevail in time t if the composition of covariates in time s were in effect.

---

[2]We specify an additive model without interaction terms. This model is simplistic because it assumes that no covariate affects y through any of the other covariates.

Based on the constructed actual marginal distribution, we can estimate any inequality measure denoted by $\hat{I}(\hat{\beta}_t; C_t)$. Similarly, based on the constructed counterfactual marginal distribution, we can estimate the corresponding measure denoted by $\hat{I}(\hat{\beta}_t; C_s)$. By comparing these measures, we arrive at a two-component decomposition:

$$\Delta \hat{I} = \hat{I}_2 - \hat{I}_1$$
$$= I(\hat{\beta}_2; C_2) - I(\hat{\beta}_1; C_1)$$
$$= \{I(\hat{\beta}_2; C_2) - I(\hat{\beta}_2; C_1)\}$$
$$+ \{I(\hat{\beta}_2; C_1) - I(\hat{\beta}_1; C_1)\}, \qquad (7.2)$$

where the estimated inequality difference is partitioned into two difference terms. The first difference term fixes coefficients at Time 2 but allows the composition of covariates to vary between the two times, thereby capturing the change in the overall inequality measure generated by the change in composition of all covariates. The second differencing term fixes the composition of covariates at Time 1 but allows the coefficients to change from Time 1 to Time 2, thereby capturing the change in the overall inequality measure generated by the change in coefficients.

The inequality measure in Equation 7.2 is based on the model-based marginal distribution. Modeling the large number (but smaller than the sample size) of quantiles helps characterize the distribution but does not re-create the distribution. Thus, we need to document the discrepancy between the observed marginal and the constructed marginal using both a graphic approach and a numerical approach. It is informative to give a graphic view and also assess the unexplained variation in the overall inequality measure:

$$I = \hat{I} + \hat{\varepsilon}.$$

The following are step-by-step descriptions of the empirical procedures we use to obtain the model-based (Procedure A) and the counterfactual-based (Procedure B) marginal samples. Both procedures lead to approximate samples from their corresponding marginal distributions based on the following idea. We sample a row of the covariate data from one time period, and plug that row into a QRM fitted for either the same time period or the other time period, for a randomly selected quantile value in (0, 1). The resulting response variable value will have the correct marginal distribution.

Procedure A consists of the following steps to approximate the model-based marginal distributions for each time t:

1. Select one U at random from the uniform distribution $U(0, 1)$.

2. Estimate the Uth QR using the complete time t data.

3. Select a bootstrap sample of size 40 from the time t data,[3] and obtain 40 predicted values based on the QRM estimates.

4. Calculate the conditional Uth quantile based on the selected rows of covariates x_t and the QR coefficients β_t^U.

5. Repeat Steps 1 to 4 for 500 times.

6. Take the values obtained in Step 5 ($500 \times 40 = 20,000$ fitted values) as a random sample from the model-based marginal distribution of y_t^*.

Procedure B consists of the following steps to approximate the model-based counterfactual marginal distributions:

1. Calculate the conditional quantile based on the previously randomly drawn rows of data at Time 1 $x_{t=1}$ and the previously estimated QR coefficients at Time 2 $\hat{\beta}_{t=2}$ to form what we take as a sample from the counterfactual marginal distribution $y^*(\hat{\beta}_{t=2}; x_{t=1})$.

2. The reverse-order counterfactual marginal can be established by using randomly drawn rows of data at Time 2 $x_{t=2}$ and the estimated QR coefficients at Time 1 $\hat{\beta}_{t=1}$ to form what we take as a sample from the counterfactual marginal distribution $y^*(\hat{\beta}_{t=1}; x_{t=2})$.

We illustrate the model-based decomposition method for inequality measures using the SIPP income data in 1991 and 2001. The covariates in the QRM for household income include race (black vs. white), education (college vs. non–college educated), and life cycle (age and age-squared). We obtain the model-based marginal distribution in 1991 and 2001, $\hat{F}(y_1, C_1)$ and $\hat{F}(y_2, C_2)$. We first assess how well the simulated marginal distribution agrees with the observed. A graphic view is informative (see Figure 7.1). For both years, the model-based kernel density curve largely retains the location, scale, and shape of the observed kernel density curve. The 1991 model-based curve slightly shifts to the right at its peak from the observed peak, indicating a slight discrepancy. The 2001 model-based curve is almost identical to the observed curve. Comparing the first three rows of Table 7.1 and Table 7.2, we see that the model-based 1991 inequality is indeed lower than the observed. This leads to a larger overall change in inequality based on the simulated data than for the observed data.

After simulating the counterfactual model-based marginal distributions for both orders $\hat{F}(y_2, C_1)$ and $\hat{F}(y_1, C_2)$, we have four simulated marginal

---

[3]The Machado and Mata method draws one row of covariates. We draw a bootstrap sample of size 40 to increase the sample size of the simulated marginal distribution.

118

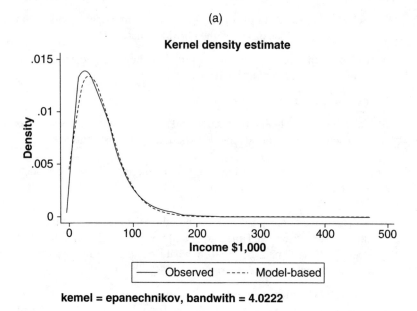

(a)

Kernel density estimate

kemel = epanechnikov, bandwith = 4.0222

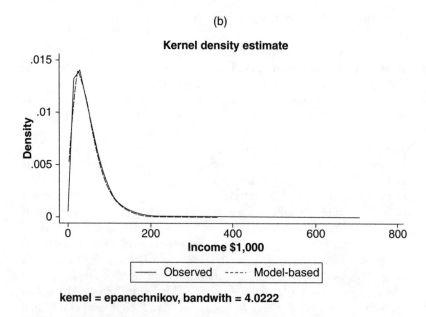

(b)

Kernel density estimate

kemel = epanechnikov, bandwith = 4.0222

Figure 7.1 Observed Versus Model-Based Marginal Distribution of Income: SIPP Data in (a) 1991 and (b) 2001

Decomposition	G	T	$A_{1/2}$
Actual 1991: $\hat{F}(y_1; C_1)$	0.362	0.215	0.111
Actual 2001: $\hat{F}(y_2; C_2)$	0.422	0.305	0.147
Overall change	0.059**	0.090**	0.036**
Counterfactual Order 1: $\hat{F}(y_2; C_1)$			
Compositional	0.004	0.008	0.003
Conditional	0.056**	0.083**	0.033**
Counterfactual Order 2: $\hat{F}(y_1; C_2)$			
Compositional	0.003	0.004	0.002
Conditional	0.056**	0.086**	0.034**
Average counterfactual Orders 1 and 2			
Compositional	0.004	0.006	0.003
Conditional	0.056**	0.084**	0.034**
Percent contribution			
Compositional	6.0	6.7	7.5
Conditional	94.0**	93.3**	92.5**

Table 7.2 Model-Based Decomposition of Income Inequality: SIPP 1991 and 2001

Note: The quantile regression models include four covariates: race (black and white), education (college and noncollege), age, and age-squared. SIPP, Survey of Income and Program Participation.

**$p < .01$.

distributions, based on which inequality measures can be calculated and decomposition analysis can be performed. We present the results for Gini coefficient G, Theil's index T, and Atkinson $A_{1/2}$. To test the significance of the trend, we use the asymptotic standard error.

Over the decade, the increase in income inequality measured by the three inequality measures is statistically significant (see the top three rows of

Table 7.2). If our QRM is correctly specified,[4] the decomposition analysis shows that the compositional change in covariates (race, education, and life cycle) does not significantly contribute to the overall increase of any of the three inequality measures. It is the conditional distribution (capturing the sorting mechanism of income) that almost completely explains the rising income inequality.

Summary

This chapter introduces methods to decompose the change in inequality between two time points into a compositional change of the covariates and the change in the conditional distribution of the response given the covariates. The method for one categorical covariate is a reweighted method, and the method for one continuous covariate or for multiple covariates is a model-based method using QR. This trend decomposition method extends our ability to analyze the sources of inequality change over time and leads to a deeper understanding of the mechanisms by which society is more divided or integrated over time. The next chapter examines income and wealth inequality in 1991 and 2001, employing most of the analytic tools introduced in this book.

---

[4]We use a simple specification here for illustration purpose only. A more realistic example can be found in Chapter 8.

CHAPTER 8. AN ILLUSTRATIVE APPLICATION

Inequality in Income and Wealth in the United States, 1991–2001

This chapter provides a real-world example of an examination of household income and wealth inequality in the United States in 1991 and 2001 using the Survey of Income and Program Participation (SIPP) data. It serves as a summary application of the tools introduced in the previous chapters. Our goal is to determine the patterns of income and wealth inequality for the total population and by social groups, and how these patterns change over the 10 years. Since income and wealth are shared within households, we take *household* as the unit of analysis. We examine income and wealth for both substantive and methodological purposes. Substantively, household resources can be conceived as *flows* captured by income and *stocks* captured by wealth. The relationship between income and wealth is a complex one. In particular, investment income and saving are examples of factors that affect this relationship. Thus, examining both income and wealth inequality can provide a more complete picture of household resource inequality. Methodologically, we apply most of the tools to the examination of income as practiced in the income literature. In the income case, we focus on positive income values because the proportion of households with negative and zero income is small. However, the investigation of wealth inequality will require a different set of tools since the proportion with negative and zero values of net worth (total assets minus total debts) is substantial. The contrast between income and wealth reminds us that the choice of appropriate tools depends on the phenomenon in question. The SIPP collects detailed information on both income and wealth, making it an appropriate source for this study. The SIPP uses a multistage cluster, stratified sampling design, and the sampled households have different sampling weights. Analyses in this example take into account sampling weights and the survey sampling design. We perform the analysis using user-written modules in Stata—ineqdeco and ineqdec0 (Jenkins, 1999), glcurve (Van Kerm & Jenkins, 2001), reldist (Jann, 2008), and DASP (Distributive Analysis Stata Program; Duclos & Arrar, 2006) (see Appendix Table 8.A1).

Descriptive Statistics

Table 8.1 shows the weighted descriptive statistics for variables used in the analysis. Annual income is calculated by summing up monthly total household income in the calendar years 1991 and 2001. We analyze annual income with positive values, excluding 53 (0.25%) households with zero income and 838 (4.02%) with missing income in 1991 (no households with negative income) and 4 (0.01%) households with negative income, and 100 (0.35%) with zero income in 2001 (no households with missing income). Because of these relatively small percentages of households with nonpositive income, eliminating them will only minimally affect income inequality patterns. In contrast, 1,751 (8.4%) households had negative net worth and 916 (4.4%) households had zero net worth in 1991. The corresponding number is 3,546 (12.9%) and 1,158 (4.2%) in 2001, portions of the total net worth distribution that we cannot ignore without affecting inequality patterns. Both income and net worth are in 2001 constant dollars, so that they can be compared over time. The first row of Table 1 shows that the mean of both income and net worth increases from 1991 to 2001.

Social structure plays an important role in determining the position of a household in terms of income and wealth. Based on social stratification theories, we identify six social grouping variables: race/ethnicity (white, black, Hispanic, other), age group (household heads older than 45 years vs. younger), education group (below high school, high school, some college, and college or above), household type (married without children, married with children, single mother, single man, single woman, and other), region (Northeast, Midwest, South, and West), and household setting (metropolitan areas or not). Comparing the "proportion" columns of Table 8.1 shows the change in population proportions of these social groups from 1991 to 2001. We see an increase in racial minority groups, the older age group, highly educated groups, unmarried household types, southern residents, and metropolitan residents. Later on, we will ask whether these compositional changes in social groupings contribute to the change in income and wealth inequality, and the degree of these contributions.

The "mean income" and "mean net worth" columns show mean values for each social group in 1991 and 2001. While all but three groups gained in income and net worth over the 10-year period, it appears that the more advantaged groups gained more, including whites, older, highest educated, married household types, single-man households, and metropolitan areas. The mean income for all educated groups but the highest dropped over time. The mean net worth of those without a high school diploma declined by a large margin, while those with a high school education and those having some college education exhibited a small increase. In contrast, college and advanced education produced the greatest boost in net worth over the 10 years. Looking at income and net worth simultaneously leads to more insight into household resources.

While these descriptive statistics are informative, they do not give a clear sense of inequality that is based on the whole distribution, so we turn to the observed inequality patterns using both graphic views and summary inequality measures.

| | 1991 | | | | 2001 | | | |
Variable	Proportion	Mean Income ($)	Mean Net Worth ($)		Proportion	Mean Income ($)	Mean Net Worth ($)	
Total	1.00	47,908	118,468		1.00	51,040	173,993	
Race/ethnicity								
White	0.80	50,609	134,857		0.75	54,168	210,377	
Black	0.10	32,190	35,391		0.12	35,797	45,472	
Hispanic	0.07	37,144	49,368		0.09	40,998	57,905	
Other race	0.03	52,660	120,371		0.04	61,419	151,915	
Age group								
Age < 45	0.49	49,155	61,968		0.45	52,687	83,292	
Age ≥ 45	0.51	46,717	173,087		0.55	49,699	247,818	
Education group								
< High school	0.23	28,728	75,755		0.14	26,541	57,946	
High school	0.35	43,406	98,923		0.30	40,387	114,691	
Some college	0.20	50,956	114,462		0.30	49,277	140,135	

(Continued)

Variable	1991				2001		
	Proportion	Mean Income ($)	Mean Net Worth ($)		Proportion	Mean Income ($)	Mean Net Worth ($)
College	0.22	72,514	199,006		0.26	78,964	345,826
Household type							
Married without kids	0.23	54,859	196,067		0.23	59,280	282,636
Married with kids	0.33	63,561	123,768		0.28	72,490	207,784
Single mom	0.10	31,483	47,476		0.11	32,983	50,835
Single man	0.10	33,560	75,756		0.11	34,695	149,631
Single woman	0.15	23,615	87,771		0.15	23,726	112,522
Other household	0.09	48,347	85,923		0.11	50,916	91,618
Region							
Northeast	0.20	51,773	144,972		0.19	55,651	185,108
Midwest	0.26	47,149	108,245		0.23	51,267	154,291
South	0.34	42,949	93,983		0.37	46,314	140,224
West	0.20	53,192	145,834		0.21	54,834	243,909

Variable	1991			2001		
	Proportion	Mean Income ($)	Mean Net Worth ($)	Proportion	Mean Income ($)	Mean Net Worth ($)
Metropolitan						
Yes	0.74	51,041	123,957	0.77	54,102	190,311
No	0.26	39,458	102,839	0.23	40,761	119,213
Continuous covariate (mean)						
Age	48			49		
Years of schooling	12.72			13.14		
Household size	2.39			2.30		
Total N	20,838			27,398		

Table 8.1 Weighted Descriptive Statistics of Income and Wealth, Total and by Social Groups: SIPP 1991 and 2001

Note: SIPP, Survey of Income and Program Participation.

Observed Income and Wealth Inequality

Graphic views aid in visualizing the entire distribution. Figure 8.1 provides the quantile functions, the Lorenz curve, and the generalized Lorenz curve for annual income in the left three figures, and the same set of graphs for net worth in the right three figures. The quantile functions, created by "pctile" in Stata, show that the 2001 curve for income and net worth departs from the corresponding 1991 curve from $p70$ and above. The departure is greater for net worth than income. This suggests that changes over time were concentrated in the upper one third of the distribution.

Using the "glcurve" module by Jenkins and Van Kerm (2004), we produce Lorenz curves and generalized Lorenz curves for 1991 and 2001. Lorenz curves are normalized by the response mean, which takes out the scale shift. Thus, we use Lorenz curves to compare the location shift and shape shift between the distributions for the 2 years. The first thing catching our eye is the much greater enclosed area between the Lorenz and the line of perfect equality for net worth than income, indicating the more severe inequality in wealth than income, as documented in the literature. Second, we see the 2001 Lorenz lying below the 1991 Lorenz for both income and net worth, suggesting that the 2001 income/wealth Lorenz dominates the 1991 income/wealth. We performed a formal test of Lorenz dominance for the 1991 and 2001 income with inequality measures that are bottom, middle, and top sensitive (GE_{-20}, GE_1, and GE_{20}; results are not shown here) and confirmed that the 2001 income distribution Lorenz dominates the 1991 income distribution. However, it is not as straightforward to do such a formal test for net worth because bottom-sensitive inequality measures cannot be used for negative values of net worth. We used GE_1 and GE_{20} for differences in the positive value portion and confirm that the positive value portion of the net worth distribution in 2001 Lorenz dominates that in 1991.

The generalized Lorenz curve is obtained by multiplying the Lorenz function with the mean income or wealth. The rescaling of the y-axis reminds us that while income and wealth inequality increased from 1991 to 2001, social welfare due to income and wealth improved over the same period.

Beyond the graphic views are the precise summary inequality measures. We choose a set of measures that give us complementary information to form a more complete picture of inequality. We use DASP by Duclos and Araar (2006) to obtain weighted income and wealth inequality measures in 1991 and 2001. Alternatively, we can use "ineqdeco" by Jenkins (1999) for income and "ineqdec0" by Jenkins for net worth. The results for each year and their absolute and relative differences are presented in the top section of Table 8.2 for income and in the bottom panel for net worth.

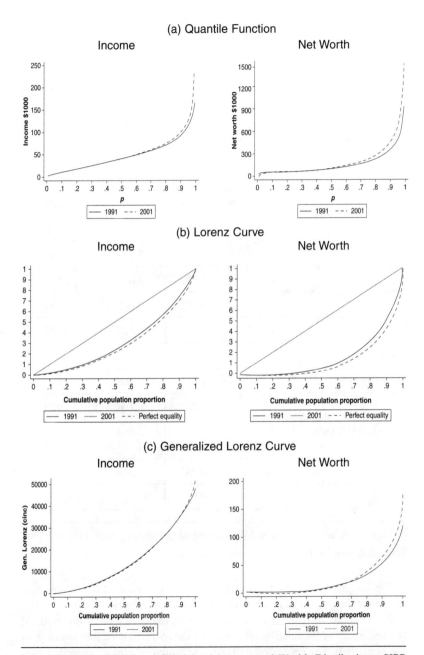

Figure 8.1 Graphic View of Weighted Income and Wealth Distributions, SIPP 1991 and 2001: (a) Quantile Function, (b) Lorenz Curve, and (c) Generalized Lorenz Curve

128

Measures	1991	2001	Change	Percentage Change
Income				
$p10/p50$	0.290	0.286	−0.004	−1.38
$p90/p50$	2.294	2.494	0.200	8.72
Gini	0.382	0.422	0.039	10.21
GE_{-1}	1.288	3.859	2.571	199.61
GE_0	0.284	0.346	0.061	21.48
GE_1	0.240	0.308	0.068	28.33
GE_2	0.265	0.404	0.139	52.45
$A_{0.5}$	0.121	0.148	0.027	22.31
A_1	0.247	0.292	0.045	18.22
A_2	0.720	0.885	0.165	22.92
Net worth				
$p75/p25$	26.464	46.224	19.760	74.67
$p90/p50$	6.715	7.421	0.706	10.51
Bottom half/top 5% share ratio	0.124	0.045	−0.080	−64.52
Gini	0.694	0.763	0.069	9.94
GE_2	1.455	40.970	39.515	2715.81

Table 8.2 Weighted Income and Wealth Inequality Measures: SIPP 1991 and 2001
Note: SIPP, Survey of Income and Program Participation.

We first examine income inequality. We begin with quantile ratios since they have the benefit of being simple to calculate and easy to interpret. The $p10/p50$ (ratio of 10th percentile to the median) describes the bulk of the lower half of the distribution, whereas the $p90/p50$ describes the bulk of the upper half. The decreased $p10/p50$ and increased $p90/p50$ together suggest the deepening of income inequality. The increased mode-sensitive Gini coefficient for income further confirms that the greater income inequality occurs for the middle portion of the distribution. We use four values of the generalized entropy sensitivity parameter (−1, 0, 1, and 2). As each parameter's value increases, the sensitivity moves from the bottom to the top of the distribution. All four generalized entropy measures exhibit an increase from 1991 to 2001, with an increase that is concentrated in the two ends rather than in the middle. The bottom-sensitive GE_{-1} exhibits an almost 200% increase, and the top-sensitive GE_2 exhibits an over 50% increase. These measures provide additional information about changes in the bottom tail of the income distribution that the quantile functions in Figure 8.1 do not capture. The Atkinson family of indexes provides an inequality aversion perspective. As the aversion becomes stronger, the level of and change in income inequality also become greater, but not the percentage change.

We now turn to the study of net worth. Because net worth can take negative values, some care is required in choosing which quantiles should be used to form ratios so as to avoid negative quantile ratios, simply because these are difficult to interpret. The $p75/p25$ ratio captures the net worth inequality among the middle 50% of the population. The wealth inequality is already large for this middle half of the population, and it grows substantially over the 10 years. The $p90/p50$ ratio is around 7 and relatively stable over time. This, together with the Lorenz curve comparison above, suggests that affluence occurs at even as low as the 90th percentile. We further examine the bottom 50% to the top 5% share ratio. Taking the whole population's wealth as a pie (sum of positive and negative values of net worth), the bottom half of the population has a much smaller piece of the pie than the top 5% of the population as their ratio is only 0.124 in 1991, which further drops to 0.045 in 2001. While the net worth Gini is much higher than the income Gini, the growth rate at about 10% is similar for both income Gini and net worth Gini. The result for GE_2 shows a huge change over the decade. Overall, the selected inequality measures in Table 8.2 indicate that both income and wealth inequality increased over the decade. However, whether these results are statistically significant are subject to hypothesis testing, which we will perform later.

Among the six social grouping variables, how do group mean differences contribute to the total inequality? Which grouping variable contributes more? Do these group contributions change over time? We use the group decomposition tool to answer this question, focusing on Gini and GE with four different sensitivity parameters. The *between* component is defined as the inequality between groups when, instead of group members having different values of wealth, within each group, members have identical values of wealth equal to the group's mean wealth. We note that in addition to capturing group mean differences, group composition is factored into this calculation, that is, the relative group sizes matter. We use DASP to produce results shown in Table 8.3. Take race/ethnicity grouping as an example. From the top section for income, the between component contributes 13.42% to Gini, very little to GE_{-1} and about 4% to GE_0, GE_1, and GE_2. These contributions by race/ethnicity are quite stable over the decade. It should be kept in mind that while the generalized entropy family is additively decomposable, Gini is not. We see that the racial/ethnic contribution to Gini is large, and it increases slightly over the 10 years. Looking across the grouping variables, we see two patterns. First, the between components of education groups and household types are the largest contributor to the total income inequality among the six grouping variables. Second, these between components' contributions change moderately over the 10-year period.

Different patterns, however, emerge for net worth (bottom section of Table 8.3). The age grouping, capturing the life cycle difference in wealth accumulation, joins education groups and household types to make a greater contribution to the total wealth inequality. Under additive decomposability, the declined contribution to GE_2 of between-group components implies that the within-group variation in the top tail plays a greater role in 2001 than in 1991. In contrast, under nonadditive decomposability, the increased contribution to Gini of between-group components (with one exception) suggests that group mean differences play a more important role for the middle portion in 2001 than in 1991.

Households have various portfolios of wealth. We focus on three categories— home equity (home value minus mortgage), financial net worth (IRA, bank accounts, stocks, and mutual funds, etc., minus collaterals) and other net worth such as real estate equity, credit card debts, and medical debts. We use DASP to perform the decomposition by sources for Gini coefficients. As Table 8.4 shows, financial net worth makes the largest percentage contribution to the total Gini, and this contribution declines from 1991 to 2001. The "other" category makes a negative percentage contribution in 1991, meaning that there are more debts than assets in this category. This turns out to be positive in 2001.

Testing Trends of Income and Wealth Inequality

We have discussed the observed patterns of various income and wealth inequality measures for the whole population and group/source decompositions of the total inequality measures. We now consider testing the significance of the trends in these measures, that is, inference about their time changes. As discussed in Chapter 6, when the sample size is large (say, greater than 1,000), the asymptotic approach is appropriate for determining the approximate sampling distribution for most summary inequality measures, under simple random sampling. However, surveys usually involve

	Race	Age	Education	Household Type	Region	Rural
Income 1991						
Gini	13.42	3.41	44.27	45.16	12.18	12.39
GE_{-1}	0.85	0.03	3.73	5.01	0.27	0.48
GE_0	3.68	0.12	17.08	20.77	1.29	2.19
GE_1	3.95	0.15	19.9	21.99	1.52	2.48
GE_2	3.25	0.13	18.19	18.26	1.37	2.14
2001						
Gini	14.85	3.63	44.24	46.62	9.81	10.91
GE_{-1}	0.32	0.01	1.66	2.21	0.08	0.18
GE_0	3.31	0.14	17.5	21.18	0.84	1.93
GE_1	3.48	0.15	19.38	21.38	0.94	2.05
GE_2	2.51	0.12	15.15	15.26	0.71	1.48
Net worth 1991						
Gini	16.22	33.41	27.07	31.46	14.63	5.35
GE_2	3.07	7.45	4.76	5.59	1.26	0.21
2001						
Gini	21.21	30.64	39.61	33.05	15.43	9.46
GE_2	0.17	0.27	0.44	0.24	0.06	0.04

Table 8.3 Weighted Percentage Contribution of Between-Group Components to Income and Wealth Inequality: SIPP 1991 and 2001

Note: SIPP, Survey of Income and Program Participation.

complex sampling designs, which must be accounted for in the asymptotic approach. For a set of commonly used summary inequality measures, we use the DASP package to perform such analyses.

Table 8.5 shows the results of testing the change over time in the same set of inequality measures shown in Table 8.2. We show the change, the

132

Section	1991	2001
Home equity	0.38	0.31
Financial net worth	0.79	0.59
Other	−0.18	0.10

Table 8.4 Weighted Percentage Contribution of Source section to Net Worth Gini: SIPP 1991 and 2001

Note: SIPP, Survey of Income and Program Participation.

p value, and the 95% confidence interval (CI) for each measure. We observe that the change in all income inequality measures in the table is significant at the .01 level, except for the change in the $p10/p50$ ratio for income and the change in GE_2 for net worth, which are statistically insignificant. In other words, the estimated minimal decline (−0.004) in the $p10/p50$ income ratio is negligible and the change in GE_2 for net worth (39.515), which appears to be great in magnitude, is the result of sampling variability. These two measures with insignificant changes will then not be further analyzed. Nonetheless, we have evidence that both income inequality and wealth inequality increase from 1991 to 2001, and this is true when we focus on the middle ($p90/p50$, Gini, GE_0, and GE_1 for income and $p75/p25$, $p90/p10$, and Gini for net worth), the bottom end (GE_{-1} for income and bottom half to top 5% share ratio for net worth), and the upper end (GE_2 for income and bottom half to top 5% share ratio for net worth).

Among the social groups examined above, the between component of educational groups has a relatively large contribution to those income and wealth inequality measures that are sensitive to the middle and the two ends (from Table 8.3). We now take a closer look at the within component of the education grouping variable. A large body of literature has established that college education has been an important source of rising social inequality since the 1980s (Bernhardt, Morris, Handcock, & Scott, 2001; Card & DiNardo, 2002; Goldin & Katz, 2007; Grogger & Eide, 1995). However, the education grouping contribution to the shape of the income and wealth distributions remains less understood. Since this question can be boiled down to a question about the shape shift in income or wealth between two educational groups, we make use of the relative distribution method. Specifically, we use the median relative polarization (MRP) and its components (lower and upper polarization) to study this problem. We ask whether and how college education contributes to the level and change

Measure	Change	p Value	LB	UB
Income				
$p10/p50$	−0.004	0.533	−0.016	0.008
$p90/p50$	0.200	0.000	0.138	0.263
Gini	0.039	0.000	0.033	0.046
GE_{-1}	2.571	0.008	0.706	4.437
GE_0	0.061	0.000	0.050	0.073
GE_1	0.068	0.000	0.057	0.079
GE_2	0.139	0.000	0.116	0.161
$A_{0.5}$	0.027	0.000	0.022	0.031
A_1	0.045	0.000	0.036	0.054
A_2	0.165	0.003	0.058	0.272
Net worth				
$p75/p25$	19.760	0.000	23.367	29.562
$p90/p50$	0.706	0.000	6.419	7.011
Bottom half/top 5% share ratio	−0.080	0.000	−0.106	−0.053
Gini	0.069	0.000	0.040	0.098
GE_2	39.515	0.192	−19.803	98.832

Table 8.5 Testing Change in Income and Wealth Inequality from 1991 to 2001: SIPP Data

Note: LB and UB stand for the lower and upper bounds of the 95% confidence interval. SIPP, Survey of Income and Program Participation.

of these measures of income and wealth polarization from 1991 to 2001. For the purpose of inference for these measures, we use the more flexible bootstrap approach because the asymptotic properties of these estimators are unknown. We also account for the complex survey sampling design in the bootstrap method. We use "reldist" by Ben Jann (2008) to perform this analysis of relative polarization.

The relative distribution analysis is conducted separately for each year for income. Because the relative distribution method can be applied to any distribution without a requirement of positive values, we are able to perform a parallel analysis for net worth. We take the college educated as the comparison group, and the non–college educated as the reference group. Since our question is about the shape shift, "reldist" first takes out the influence of the median difference by making the non-college-educated group median aligned with the college-educated group. Then "reldist" performs the grade transformation to produce the median-adjusted relative data, based on which MRP and its two components—lower relative polarization (LRP) and upper relative polarization (URP)—are calculated (weighted MRP, LRP, and URP are used). The bootstrap standard error (BSE) of MRP, LRP, and URP can be obtained accounting for clustering and stratification in the SIPP survey design. The analysis makes use of 200 bootstrap repetitions. To construct Table 8.6, we use the weighted MRP, LRP, and URP and the BSEs for 1991 and 2001 obtained from "reldist" in three additional steps. First, we construct the 95% CI for MRP, LRP, and URP in each year: 95% CI = weighted estimate $\pm$ 1.96 $\times$ BSE. Second, we subtract the weighted MRP, LRP, and URP in 1991 from those in 2001 to yield the changes between the 2 years. Third, we calculate the standard error for the changes using $\sqrt{BSE^2_{1991} + BSE^2_{2001}}$ (polarization measures in the two years are assumed to be uncorrelated).

The top section presents the results for income. For 1991, the MRP is 0.2583, meaning that 25.83% of the college educated are relatively more polarized when compared with the non–college graduated. The greater LRP than URP indicates that, in comparison with the non–college educated, the lower half of the college educated are much more spread out than the upper half. Specifically, 16.22% (32.43%/2) of the college educated have moved farther to the left from the median, whereas 9.62% (19.23%/2) of the college educated have moved farther to the right from the median. It should be noted that we are focusing on the shape difference, and the median difference is already removed. All three measures of polarization are significantly different from 0 as shown by the BSEs and 95% CI.

The relative income polarization measures between the two educational groups all increase substantially from 1991 to 2001. In particular, a 27% increase in the LRP (0.0882/0.3243 = 0.27) tops a 23% increase in MRP and a 16% increase in URP, indicating a more serious contraction of the lower half of the non–college educated in the income distribution. All three changes are statistically significant at the .01 level.

The bottom section of Table 8.6 presents results for net worth. It is not surprising that the median relative polarization by education is more serious for wealth than for income. About 47.10% of the college

Measure	Estimate	BSE	LB	UB
Income 1991				
MRP	0.2583	0.0084	0.2419	0.2748
LRP	0.3243	0.0134	0.2980	0.3506
URP	0.1923	0.0101	0.1726	0.2121
2001				
MRP	0.3175	0.0070	0.3038	0.3311
LRP	0.4125	0.0109	0.3912	0.4338
URP	0.2224	0.0084	0.2059	0.2390
Change				
MRP	0.0592**	0.0109		
LRP	0.0882**	0.0172		
URP	0.0301**	0.0131		
Net worth 1991				
MRP	0.4710	0.0111	0.4494	0.4927
LRP	0.6592	0.0205	0.6190	0.6994
URP	0.2829	0.0094	0.2644	0.3013
2001				
MRP	0.5529	0.0056	0.5419	0.5640
LRP	0.7516	0.0098	0.7324	0.7708
URP	0.3543	0.0070	0.3406	0.3679
Change				
MRP	0.0819**	0.0124		
LRP	0.0924**	0.0227		
URP	0.0714**	0.0117		

Table 8.6 Testing Changes in Weighted Relative Polarization by College Education From 1991 to 2001: SIPP Data

Note: BSE, bootstrap standard error; LRP, lower relative polarization; MRP, median relative polarization; SIPP, Survey of Income and Program Participation; URP, upper relative polarization. LB and UB stand for the lower and upper bounds of the 95% confidence interval.

**p < .01.

educated move toward the two distribution tails compared with the non–college educated. The contraction in the lower half of the non-college-educated distribution is the main source of this difference. While the relative polarization of wealth deepens in 2001, as does the income relative polarization, the rate of change is greater in the upper half (a 25% increase) versus a 17% increase in MRP and a 14% increase in LRP. Thus, the wealthy college educated become increasingly wealthier over the decade. These changes are statistically significant at the .01 level.

Decomposing Trends of Income and Wealth Inequality

Results from the last section confirm that many inequality measures for income and wealth significantly differ over the 10-year period. Inequality measures are determined by both the sorting mechanism, either by social structure or by luck, and the composition of the characteristics of the population. Holding the sorting mechanism constant, a change in the composition of race/ethnicity, age, education, household types, and other characteristics would change income and wealth inequality. Likewise, holding the compositions of these characteristics constant, a change in the sorting mechanism would also change the landscape of inequality. Thus, a next logical question is how to quantify the relative contribution of these two components.

Examining inequality using one predictor variable at a time is problematic because there is more than one population covariate, and these covariates are correlated with each other. For example, blacks are more likely to be less educated, live in single-mother households, or live in the South. Thus, a multivariate regression framework is needed. Quantile regression models (QRMs) have advantages over linear regression models when we need to look at the whole distribution and perform trend decomposition. We apply the Machado and Mata (2005) method to both income and net worth inequality trend decomposition. Our QRM specification includes 16 covariates: 3 dummy variables for race/ethnicity, age and age squared, years of education, 5 dummy variables for 6 types of households, household size, 3 dummy variables for region, and metropolitan area.

Using income as an example, we perform the following procedures (as in Chapter 7).

Procedure A. Simulate the QRM-implied marginal income distribution for 1991 and 2001, respectively.

1. Select one U at random from the uniform distribution $U(0, 1)$.

2. Estimate the Uth QRM using the 1991 data.[1]

3. Select a bootstrap sample of size 40 from the 1991 data and obtain the predicted income based on the QRM estimates.

4. Repeat Steps 1 to 3 for 500 times.

5. Stack the predicted income values to obtain a random sample of the 1991 marginal income distribution implied by the QRM (for 500 different quantiles) with a size of $500 \times 40 = 20,000$.

6. Repeat Steps 1 to 5, substituting the 1991 data with the 2001 data.

Procedure B. Simulate the counterfactual marginal income distribution using the 2001 QRM coefficients and the 1991 data on covariates (Counterfactual Order 1). Simulate the reverse-order counterfactual marginal income distribution using the 1991 QRM coefficients and the 2001 data on covariates (Counterfactual Order 2).

Based on the 1991 marginal and the 2001 marginal, we obtain the overall change in an inequality measure (the third row of Table 8.7). For each counterfactual order, the compositional and conditional components for an inequality measure are obtained using the method described in Chapter 7 (see Equation 7.2). Taking the average of the results based on each counterfactual order, we obtain the final result for the compositional and conditional components (the last two rows of Table 8.7).

In Table 8.7, the $p90/p50$ based on the marginal distributions (implied by the QRM) increased over the decade from 2.115 to 2.287, indicating that the rich became richer. The estimates of the two components differ between the two counterfactual orderings. The decomposition results show that the change in covariate composition has no significant effect on the 90th percentile income relative to the median income. Thus, the conditional distribution given the covariates included in the model accounts for 110.4% of the lowered $p90/p50$ ratio. In other words, the sorting mechanism completely explains the rising inequality measured by the $p10/p50$ ratio.

Turning to Gini, Theil, and GE_2, we see from their average results that the conditional distribution given the covariates drives the increase in

---

[1]In our *Quantile Regression* book (Hao & Naiman, 2007), a measure of goodness of fit denoted by $R(p)$ for the fitted pth quantile regression model is discussed. We note here that for the fitted QRM the R is 0.1543 at $p10$ and 0.2573 at $p90$, indicating that the model explains more variation in the upper tail than in the lower tail. All estimated coefficients are in the expected directions and most covariates are statistically significant.

Decomposition	p90/p50	G	GE_{-1}	GE_0	T	GE_2	$A_{1/2}$	A_1	A_2
Actual 1991: $\hat{F}(y_1; C_1)$	2.115	0.367	1.262	0.289	0.224	0.237	0.117	0.251	0.716
Actual 2001: $\hat{F}(y_2; C_2)$	2.287	0.390	1.371	0.316	0.256	0.295	0.130	0.271	0.733
Overall change	0.172**	0.023**	0.108	0.027**	0.032**	0.058**	0.013**	0.020**	0.016
Counterfactual Order 1: $\hat{F}(y_2; C_1)$									
Compositional	−0.052	−0.009**	−1.025	−0.021**	−0.013**	−0.017	−0.007**	−0.015*	−0.095
Conditional	0.223**	0.032**	1.134	0.047**	0.045**	0.076**	0.020**	0.035**	0.035
Counterfactual Order 2: $\hat{F}(y_1; C_2)$									
Compositional	0.016	−0.004	−0.445**	−0.012*	−0.006	−0.006	−0.003*	−0.009*	−0.096**
Conditional	0.156**	0.027**	0.553**	0.039**	0.038**	0.064**	0.016**	0.029**	0.112**

Decomposition	p90/p50	G	GE_{-1}	GE_0	T	GE_2	$A_{1/2}$	A_1	A_2
Average Counterfactual Orders 1 and 2									
Compositional	−0.018	−0.006	−0.735	−0.017*	−0.009	−0.011	−0.005*	−0.012	−0.095
Conditional	0.189**	0.029**	0.843	0.043**	0.041**	0.070**	0.018**	0.032**	0.073
Percentage contribution									
Compositional	−10.4	−28.4	−677.8	−62.0*	−28.4	−19.7	−38.8*	−61.5*	−578.8
Conditional	110.4**	128.4**	777.8	162.0**	128.4**	119.7**	138.8**	161.5**	446.5

Table 8.7. Model-Based Decomposing Income Trends to Compositional and Conditional Components: SIPP 1991 and 2001

Note: The quantile regression models include 16 covariates (see text for details). SIPP, Survey of Income and Program Participation.

*$p < .05$; **$p < .01$.

income inequality over the decade. The variability of the GE_{-1} estimates is high and hence the results are not statistically significant. (This greater variability of bottom-sensitive measures was discussed in Chapter 6 informed by our Monte Carlo results.) GE_0, $A_{1/2}$, and A_1 exhibit a more dramatic pattern. The change in the covariate composition significantly *reduced* income inequality measured by these indexes, while the change in the conditional distribution increased the inequality by 162% for GE_0, 138.8% for $A_{1/2}$, and 161.5% for A_1. Estimates of A_2 are highly imprecise, and hence, we do not detect significant results. Taken together, Table 8.7 shows that the covariate compositions are not responsible for the rising income inequality, and for three out of nine indexes, they may decrease inequality. In contrast, the conditional distribution given covariates, reflecting the sorting mechanism by social structure, is responsible for the rising income inequality in seven out of nine indexes examined.

The QRM specification for net worth includes the same 16 covariates in the income QRM. The net worth distribution is highly nonnormal with a substantial proportion of households having negative or zero values. The QRM has the flexibility to fit data from nonnormal distributions, as is the case with net worth. The QRM goodness of fit for net worth is lower than that for income. The goodness of fit increases with the quantiles, ranging from 0.01 to 0.21. We use Procedures A and B (described above) to analyze the net worth trend measured by the $p90/p50$ ratio and the Gini. Table 8.8 shows an increase in overall wealth inequality over the decade. Both orderings of counterfactuals stress the greater importance of the conditional distribution given covariates than the covariate composition. The change in the covariate composition reduced the $p90/p50$ ratio and has no significant effect on the Gini. In contrast, the change in the sorting mechanism of wealth increases the $p90/p50$ ratio by 152% and the Gini by 107.3%. These findings are consistent with those for income inequality. Thus, for both income and wealth, the main driving force of rising inequality is the increasingly unequal allocation of resources to social groups.

Summary

This chapter provides an illustrative example that examines inequality of income and wealth using data from a nationally representative sample of American households in 1991 and 2001. Income and wealth are two pillars of households' resources, and they feed into each other. Our joint examination of income and wealth inequality reveals a significant, substantial increase in most inequality measures for both income and wealth from 1991 to 2001. It further reveals that education groups and household types are

Decomposition	p90/p50	G
Actual 1991: $\hat{F}(y_1;C_1)$	5.389	0.678
Actual 2001: $\hat{F}(y_2;C_2)$	6.801	0.867
Overall change	1.413**	0.189**
Counterfactual Order 1: $\hat{F}(y_2;C_1)$		
Compositional	−0.586*	−0.007
Conditional	1.998**	0.196**
Counterfactual Order 2: $\hat{F}(y_1;C_2)$		
Compositional	−0.884*	−0.021*
Conditional	2.296**	0.210**
Average Counterfactual Orders 1 and 2		
Compositional	−0.735*	−0.014
Conditional	2.147**	0.203**
Percentage contribution		
Compositional	−52.0*	−7.3
Conditional	152.0**	107.3**

Table 8.8 Model-Based Decomposing Wealth Trends to Compositional and Conditional Components: SIPP 1991 and 2001

Note: The quantile regression models include 16 covariates (see text for details). SIPP, Survey of Income and Program Participation.

*$p < .05$; **$p < .01$.

more important social groupings than race/ethnicity in sorting households to different positions on the income and wealth distribution. In particular, income and wealth are more polarized in 2001 than in 1991 for the college educated than for the non–college educated. In contrast, the contraction of the non–college educated in the lower half reflects the stagnation of income

142

and wealth of the less skilled. Finally by decomposing the trends, the example concludes that the main driving force of the increased income and wealth inequality is the more unequal allocation system rather than the change in social group compositions.

The example employs most of the methodological tools introduced in the book to answer the central question about income and wealth inequality for the whole population and by social groups. These tools as a whole provide the means for a systematic investigation into inequality. We now know how to make visual views of inequality measures, choose a limited set of inequality measures to stress different parts of the distribution or levels of inequality aversion that are relevant to the response variable, test hypotheses about trends, decompose total inequality by groups or sources, and decompose trends into compositional and distributional components. The four principles of inequality measures and the Lorenz dominance provide guidance for comparisons of either cross-time patterns or between-group patterns. The relationship between quantile functions and Lorenz curves helps distinguish location shifts from shape shifts in summary inequality measures, quantile-based measures, and relative distribution-based measures. QRMs allow for model-based decomposition of trends and pinpoint what is the engine of the increasing income and wealth inequality.

Our example also illustrates that when dealing with response variables with many negative and zero values, we face greater constraints on the types of tools appropriate for use. Greater care is demanded for these variables as we showed in the example of net worth. With both substantive and methodological illustrations, we end this chapter and the book. We hope that the book will assist our readers in gaining greater knowledge and engaging in research on the patterns, sources, and consequences of social inequality.

Appendix

-glcurve-	Van Kerm and Jenkins (2001)
-inequal7-	Van Kerm (2001)
-ineqdeco-, -ineqdec0-	Jenkins (1999)
-reldist-	Jann (2008)
Various commands in DASP	Duclos and Araar (2006)

Table 8.A1 Modules and Packages in Stata for Inequality Measures

REFERENCES

Allison, P. D. (1978). Measures of inequality. *American Sociological Review, 43,* 865–880.

Atkinson, A. B. (1970). On the measurement of inequality. *Journal of Economic Theory, 2,* 244–263.

Atkinson, A. B. (1985). *The economics of inequality* (3rd ed.). Oxford, UK: Clarendon Press.

Autor, D., Katz, L. F., & Kearney, M. S. (2005). *Trends in U.S. wage inequality: Re-assessing the revisionists* (Working Paper No. 11627). Cambridge, MA: National Bureau of Economic Research.

Bernhardt, A., Morris, M., Handcock, M. S., & Scott, M. A. (2001). *Divergent paths: Economic mobility in the new American labor market.* New York: Russell Sage Foundation.

Biewen, M. (2002). Bootstrap inference for inequality, mobility and poverty measurement. *Journal of Econometrics, 8,* 317–342.

Biewen, M., & Jenkins, S. P. (2006). Variance estimation for Generalized Entropy and Atkinson inequality indices: The complex survey data case. *Oxford Bulletin of Economics and Statistics, 68*(3), 371–383.

Blau, P. M. (1977). *Inequality and heterogeneity: A primitive theory of social structure.* New York: Free Press.

Buchinsky, M. (1994). Changes in the U.S. wage structure 1963–1987: Application of quantile regression. *Econometrica, 62,* 405–458.

Burr, D. (1994). A comparison of certain bootstrap confidence intervals in the Cox model. *Journal of the American Statistical Association, 89,* 1290–1302.

Card, D., & DiNardo, J. E. (2002). Skill-biased technological change and rising wage inequality: Some problems and puzzles. *Journal of Labor Economics, 20,* 733–783.

Cowell, F. A. (2000). *Measuring inequality* (3rd ed.). London: Prentice Hall/Harvester Wheatsheaf. Retrieved December 14, 2009, from http://darp.lse.ac.uk/papersDB/Cowell_measuring inequality3.pdf

Dalton, H. (1920). The measurement of the inequality of incomes. *Economic Journal, 30,* 348–361.

Dagum, C. (1997). A new approach to the decomposition of the Gini income inequality ratio. *Empirical Economics, 22,* 515–531.

Deaton, A. (1997). *The analysis of household surveys.* Baltimore: Johns Hopkins University Press for the World Bank.

DiNardo, J., Fortin, N., & Lemieux, T. (1996). Labor market institutions and the distribution of wages, 1973–1992: A semiparametric approach. *Econometrica, 64,* 1001–1044.

Duclos, J. Y., & Araar, A. (2006). *Poverty and equity: Measurement, policy and estimation with DAD.* Retrieved December 14, 2009, from www.idrc.ca/openebooks/229-5

Efron, B. (1979). Bootstrap methods: Another look at the jackknife. *Annals of Statistics, 7*(1), 1–26.

Efron, B., & Tibshirani, R. (1986). Bootstrap methods for standard errors, confidence intervals, and other measures of statistical accuracy. *Statistical Science, 1,* 54–77.

Efron, B., & Tibshirani, R. (1993). *An introduction to the bootstrap.* New York: Chapman & Hall.

Firebaugh, G. (1999). Empirics of world income inequality. *American Journal of Sociology, 104,* 1597–1630.

Foster, J. F., & Ok, E. A. (1999). Lorenz dominance and the variance of logarithms. *Econometrica, 67*(4), 901–907.

Fraley, C., & Raftery, A. E. (1998). How many clusters? Which clustering methods? Answers via model-based clustering analysis. *Computer Journal, 41,* 578–588.

144

Goldin, C., & Katz, L. F. (2007). *Long-run changes in the U.S. wage structure: Narrowing, widening, polarizing* (NBER Working Papers 13568). Cambridge, MA: National Bureau of Economic Research.

Grogger, J., & Eide, E. (1995). Changes in college skills and the rise in the college wage premium. *Journal of Human Resources, 30,* 280–310.

Hall, P. (1992). *Bootstrap and Edgeworth expansion.* New York: Springer-Verlag.

Handcock, M. S., & Morris, M. (1999). *Relative distribution methods in the social sciences.* New York: Springer.

Hao, L. X., & Naiman, D. Q. (2007). *Quantile regression.* Thousand Oaks, CA: Sage.

Jann, B. (2008). *reldist: Stata module for relative distribution analysis.* Unpublished manuscript. (Available on request from the author, jannb@ethz.ch)

Jenkins, S. P. (1999). *INEQDECO: Stata module to estimate a range of inequality and related indices, plus optional decompositions of a subset of these indices by population subgroup* (Statistical Software Components S432001). Boston: Department of Economics, Boston College. Retrieved January 4, 2010, from http://ideas.repec.org/c/boc/bocode/s366002.html

Jenkins, S. P., & Van Kerm, P. (2004). *GLCURVE: Stata module to generate generalized Lorenz curve* (Statistical Software Components s366302). Boston: Department of Economics, Boston College. Retrieved January 4, 2010, from http://ideas.repec.org/c/boc/bocode/s366302.html

Jenkins, S. P., & Van Kerm, P. (2005). Accounting for income distribution trends: A density function decomposition approach. *Journal of Economic Inequality, 3*(1), 43–61.

Jolliffe, D., & Krushelnytsky, B. (1999). sg115. *INEQERR: Stata model to compute bootstrap standard errors for indices of inequality. Stata Technical Bulletin, 51,* 28–32.

Juhn, C., Murphy, K. M., & Pierce, B. (1993). Wage inequality and the rise in returns to skill. *Journal of Political Economy, 101*(3), 410–442.

Koenker, R. (2005). *Quantile regression.* Cambridge, MA: Cambridge University Press.

Kolm, S. (1969). The optimal production of social justice. In J. Margolis & H. Guitton (Eds.), *Public economics* (pp. 145–200). London: Macmillan.

Kullback, S., & Leibler, R. A. (1951). On information and sufficiency. *Annals of Mathematical Statistics, 22,* 79–86.

Lambert, P. J., & Aroson, J. R. (1993). Inequality decomposition analysis and the Gini coefficient revisited. *Economic Journal, 103*(420), 1221–1227.

Lerman, R. I., & Yitzhaki, S. (1984). A note on the calculation and interpretation of the Gini Index. *Economic Letters, 15,* 363–368.

Liao, T. F. (2006). Measuring and analyzing class inequality with the Gini Index informed by model-based clustering. *Sociological Methodology, 36,* 201–224.

Liao, T. F. (2009). *Conceptualizing and measuring structural inequality* (Working Paper 2009–03). New Haven, CT: The Center for Research on Inequalities and Life Course, Yale University.

Lopez-Feldman, A. (2006). DESCOGINI: Decomposing inequality and obtaining marginal effects. *Stata Journal, 6,* 106–111.

Lorenz, M. C. (1905). Methods of measuring the concentration of wealth. *Publications of the American Statistical Association, 9,* 209–219.

Machado, J., & Mata, J. (2005). Counterfactual decompositions of changes in wage distributions using quantile regression. *Journal of Applied Econometrics, 20,* 445–465.

Mooney, C. Z., & Duval, R. D. (1993). *Bootstrapping: A nonparametric approach to statistical inference.* Newbury Park, CA: Sage.

Mussard, S., Terraza, M., & Seyte, F. (2003). Decomposition of Gini and the generalized entropy inequality measures. *Economics Bulletin, 4,* 1–5.

Neyman, J., & Pearson, E. (1933). On the problem of the most efficient tests of statistical hypotheses. *Philosophical Transactions of the Royal Society of London, Series A: Containing Papers of a Mathematical or Physical Character, 231,* 289–337.

Oaxaca, R. (1973). Male-female wage differentials in urban labor markets. *International Economic Review, 14,* 693–709.

Pen, J. (1973). A parade of dwarfs (and a few giants). In A. B. Atkinson (Ed.), *Wealth, income and inequality* (pp. 73–82). London, UK: Penguin Books.

Sastry, D. V. S., & Kelkar, U. R. (1994). Note on the decomposition of Gini inequality. *Review of Economics and Statistics, 76*(3), 584–586.

Sen, A. K. (1973). *On economic inequality.* Oxford, UK: Clarendon Press.

Sen, A. K. (1976). Poverty: An ordinal approach to measurement. *Econometrica, 44,* 219–231.

Shorrocks, A. F. (1980). The class of additively decomposable inequality measures. *Econometrica, 48,* 613–625.

Shorrocks, A. F., & Slottje, D. (2002). Approximating unanimity orderings: An application to Lorenz dominance. In P. Moyes, C. Seidl, & A. Shorrocks (Eds.), *Inequalities: Theory, experiments and applications* (pp. 91–118). Vienna: Springer.

Soofi, E. S. (1994). Capturing the intangible concept of information. *Journal of the American Statistical Association, 89,* 1243–1254.

Van Kerm, P. (2001). *INEQUAL7: Stata module to compute measures of inequality* (Statistical Software Components S416401). Boston: Boston College Department of Economics. Retrieved January 4, 2010, from http://ideas.repec.org/c/boc/bocode/s416401.html

Van Kerm, P., & Jenkins, S. P. (2001). GLCURVE: Stata module to produce Generalized Lorenz curves and related graphs. *Stata Journal, 1,* 107–112.

INDEX